Rober

W9-DHK-039

The Black Book of American Intervention in Chile

13
29 Visas delayed
40 pre-election coup fell through
* 41 US mil'y support
† 43 CIA role secondary; Pentagon act
59 Chile will be C controlled
87 " to be strangled slowly as an example.
89 Summary.
109 treaty for disputed settlement
111 publicly nice to Chile; to cover bad
120 financed truck strike private.
122 Allende strengthened as Polls
126 Pentagon plan of 1970

ARMANDO URIBE

the black book

of American
Intervention
in Chile

Translated from the Spanish by Jonathan Casart

Beacon Press   Boston

French text © Éditions du Seuil, 1974

First published in France by Éditions du Seuil under
the title *Le Livre Noir de l'Intervention Américaine
au Chili*

English translation copyright © 1975 by Beacon Press

Beacon Press books are published under the auspices
of the Unitarian Universalist Association

Published simultaneously in hardcover and paperback editions

Simultaneous publication in Canada by Saunders of Toronto, Ltd.

All rights reserved

Printed in the United States of America

9 8 7 6 5 4 3 2 1

Excerpt from Pablo Neruda's "I Wish the Woodcutter Would Wake
Up" reprinted from *Neruda and Vallejo: Selected Poems* by permission of Robert Bly. Copyright © 1971 by Robert Bly.

"U.S. Navy's Visa Requests Worry Chile" by Tad Szulc, September 5,
1970. © 1970 by the New York Times Company. Reprinted by
permission.

Excerpt from WNET's transcript of "Who invited us?" Reprinted with
permission from WNET/13 © Educational Broadcasting Corporation
Febrary, 1970.

Library of Congress Cataloging in Publication Data

Uribe Arce, Armando.
    The black book of American intervention in Chile.
    Translation of El libro negro de la intervención
norteamericana en Chile.
    1. Chile—History—Coup d'état, 1973.
2. Chile—Foreign relations—United States.
3. United States—Foreign relations—Chile.
I. Title.
F3100.U7413   983'.064   74-16672
ISBN 0-8070-0246-1
ISBN 0-8070-0247-X (pbk.)

What we love is your peace, not your mask.
Your warrior's face is not handsome.
North America, you are handsome and spacious.

PABLO NERUDA
From "I Wish the Woodcutter Would Wake Up"
Translated by Robert Bly

AUTHOR'S NOTE

Perhaps you will be surprised that I know so much or so little. I'll explain who I am and how I learned what I tell here.

When I was eight years old, in 1942, I entered an English school in the archdiocese of Santiago. In 1944, the archbishop sold the school to the Congregation of the Holy Cross, which operates Notre Dame University. There, on Pedro Valdivia Street, I began to learn all about the United States.

After finishing high school in 1950, I entered the University of Chile and studied law. In 1954 my father, a professor of law specializing in mining disputes, was named Minister of Mines. It is his experience with Henry Holland and the copper mines which is discussed in this book; I am the witness mentioned.

I graduated from law school, received a fellowship to study in Rome, and then worked in Santiago for some years. Toward the middle of 1964 I was hired by Michigan State University, through the Fulbright program, and taught graduate courses on nationalism in the works of Latin American writers and poets. It was at Michigan State that I met the president of the university, John Hannah, who was director of AID under Nixon, and several professors who had advised Diem in Saigon; that's why this university is mentioned. I was asked to stay on, but instead returned to Chile after spending all my money on a trip to New York — a city which horrified me.

Between 1965 and 1967 (since I was legal advisor for the Chilean Atomic Energy Commission and a specialist in nuclear disarmament), I was appointed to the council of governors of the International Atomic Energy Organization, and made several trips to Vienna. I was also, during this time, Chile's delegate to the Nuclear Disarmament Conference of Latin America, which took place in Mexico. I signed, with plenipotentiary powers, the Treaty for the Prohibition of Nuclear Arms in Latin America. I began to meet American diplomats and to further my understanding of U.S. foreign policy.

In 1966 I received a letter from Dr. Henry Kissinger inviting me to Harvard's International Seminar, which he directed. I turned down the invitation, but had already started to study the professor's writings.

Foreign Minister Gabriel Valdés offered me, in 1967, the position of counselor in one of six new posts recently created by law, corresponding to my specialty. I entered Chile's Ministry of Foreign Affairs as a career diplomat, and was director of information and culture, director of international relations, and in 1968 became director general.

I was a delegate to the United Nations General Assembly in 1967 and again in 1968 and 1969, where I took part in the work of the Legal and the Political commissions. Here I learned more about the United States and what it did and undid in Chile as well as in the rest of the world. In April and May 1968 I led the Chilean delegation, as ambassador, at the extraordinary session of the United Nations to examine the Treaty for the Nonproliferation of Nuclear Arms. I had learned a great deal about disarmament and nuclear strategy. We helped to make changes in the treaty, but we did not sign it.

While I was in New York, the secretary-general of the United Nations hired me as an expert to put together a report on the Guarantees of the Nuclear Powers to the Nonnuclear Powers. It circulated as an official document at the 1968 Conference of Nonnuclear Countries in Geneva. By then, I knew a lot more about global strategy.

At the end of that year, I became counselor for the Chilean embassy in Washington, where I remained until October 10, 1970. It was quite an experience. I have personally seen and heard everything I recount in this book about the things that happened during those years. I saw and heard Nixon many times while I was chargé d'affaires *ad interim* and counselor; and naturally, on all of those occasions in Washington mentioned here. I saw Dr. Kissinger several times, and was present at Gabriel Valdés's interview with Nixon, Kissinger, and others at the White House. I knew all of the Americans mentioned in this book; I witnessed the things discussed, and many more besides. I made several trips to Chile during that time; for example, I was a delegate to the ministers' conference at Viña del Mar, which drafted the Latin American Consensus.

I participated in most of the events that happened before the Chilean presidential elections in 1970 which are recorded here, such as the Navy Band incident and other sinister episodes.

Back in Chile, between the September 4 elections and Allende's ratification by Congress, I worked with Minister Valdés on the diplomatic communication regarding the incidents connected with the dismantling of the American station on Easter Island. Later on, I served as an aide to Secretary Meyer at the transferal of office. The Allende government assigned me the task of studying the military relations between the United States and Chile. I soon had to discontinue that study because the Senate called me, as a professor of law, to serve as advisor to the Commission on Constitution, Justice and Law for the procedure of the constitutional amendment for the nationalization of copper. I worked on it for several months, and learned more about the United States and its work.

The government designated me — as a career man — Chile's first ambassador to Peking. I left Chile in July 1971. When I arrived in China, Kissinger had just departed. During my first long interview with Chou En-lai — from half-past eleven at night until almost four the next morning — the premier mentioned to me some of the American's ideas; I went further into this with Chiao Kuan-hua.

It may seem odd, but in 1971 Peking offered a prime seat for studying U. S. world policy. I was there when Nixon visited that city, while the United States was attacking and bombing neighboring countries. In a way, I could follow American foreign policy better there than in Washington.

I returned to Chile in 1972 and 1973. The last time I remained two months, in March and April, working in the Ministry of Foreign Affairs precisely on the United States and its dangerous policies.

The September military coup caught me passing through Europe. Two days before, I had met with Foreign Minister Almeyda, just back from Algiers.

All the Chilean memoranda and reports reproduced here are either my own work at different periods or work in which I participated. After careful consideration I have come to the conclusion that I am not betraying any obligations or values by publishing them. There is a higher value that spurs me on: to help my people in their resistance, and to help my country to survive.

None of Chile's permanent interests are affected by this accusation against the acts of American imperialism and its accomplices in Chile; they worked hand in hand, trying to destroy my country, its tradition, and its future.

I know well each and every one of the Chileans I name, and I regret knowing some of them. Yet, I feel that I must speak about what they have done.

I did not belong to any political party until October 1971. At that time, while I was an ambassador, I decided to join the Christian Left in order to fulfil a moral, political, and social debt to Chile's poor for the privileges my education gave me and for other advantages I had enjoyed, thanks to their hard work.

I rejected the junta. When they heard this — I was in Rome at the time — they dismissed me from my post as ambassador and, later on, put an end to my career as a diplomat. Am I still a lawyer, an honorary professor of the University of Chile, and all the other things I was in Chile? I doubt it. If they could stop me from being a writer, a friend of my friends, a Chilean, and a human being, they would do it.

I feel sorry for the military and their friends. More important, however, are my obligations to those who are persecuted and oppressed, to those disinherited Chileans whose only crime is that they are Chileans.

Let them say whatever they please against me. Let the United States do what it pleases. My answer and my epitaph, the explanation for this book and for my life now, are contained in the words of the poet, when he reached the middle of his life's road:

Tal mi face la bestia senza pace.

Paris, November 1973.

The aim of the coup on September 11, 1973, was to destroy the Chilean state — to deprive that country of its sovereign independence once and for all.

Two powerful forces worked hand in hand to achieve that end: the United States government and the traitors on the Chilean armed forces. Without their joint effort the coup could not have succeeded, and Salvador Allende would not have been killed. These renegade generals represent a class that, in order to survive, undermined its own country and deliberately allied itself with United States imperialism. Washington had to destroy Chile as a nation and as a state because it had stood for defiance of the system.

Today, the Chilean people's resistance to fascism and imperialism is an expression of their historical will to be a sovereign nation.

And yet, what is at stake in Chile concerns the whole world. The United States needs very much to prove that the Chilean model, in which a state attempts through democratic means to stand on its own outside the imperialist system, is not possible — either in Chile or in the rest of the world.

What happened in Chile is part of Washington D.C.'s global strategy. That's why the United States intervened.

This is the Black Book of that intervention.

1

In 1823, when President James Monroe formulated his country's first global doctrine, *America for the Americans*, a Chilean, who traded in the ports of the Pacific, wrote to a friend: "Yes, but we'd better watch out. As far as North Americans are concerned, *they* are the only Americans."

The man's name was Diego Portales. Today Chile's junta generals and extreme reactionaries regard him as their great political forefather. Yet they are cautious about recalling that phrase, for Portales then represented a nascent national bourgeoisie whose interests already clashed with those of the North Americans. There is nothing nationalistic about Chile's bourgeoisie today. The military rebels and the United States understand each other perfectly. For them, Portales is the patron saint of businessmen.

For nineteenth-century Chile, taking its first steps toward industrialization, the British Empire was both its main enemy and its main trading partner. The United States was merely a secondary problem. The British fleet was more of an immediate threat; North American interests seemed far away. However, in 1879, when Chile's embryonic bourgeoisie challenged Peru and Bolivia over the control of the nitrate mines (one of the most profitable monopolies of the time), it came into direct confrontation with the United States. Private U. S. interests, commencing their broad imperialistic expansion into the hemisphere, used the then-secretary of state, James G. Blaine, as a means to wedge their way into this lucrative enterprise under the pretext of "mediating" the war which

1

Chile already practically had won. In spite of quasi-armed threats, Chile's ruling class refused to share its profits with the United States.

Yet, right after the War of the Pacific, during the same decade 1880–1890, this same ruling class was prepared to put itself into the hands of British imperialism — a system even more powerful and authoritarian. Through validation of the nitrate mining certificates held by a British officer, Colonel North, and other merchants, the Chilean nitrate industry was denationalized in a very short time. In 1889–90, when President José Manuel Balmaceda — the last great defender of a national bourgeois spirit — tried to reassert Chile's rights to the nitrate as well as to the political and economic leadership of the country, the majority of the bourgeoisie, along with the more backward agrarian sectors of the country, allied with the British imperialists, and in 1891 plunged the country into a civil war which defeated the nationalist president. Balmaceda aptly described the phenomenon in his *Political Testament*, and on September 18, 1891, the day which marked the end of his presidential mandate, he committed suicide rather than live with Chile's disgrace.

In that struggle the Chilean plutocracy had been backed by two forces: their own reactionary navy and the interests of British imperialism.

A few weeks later, the United States took advantage of Chile's disgrace. Under the pretext of a ridiculous incident involving the supposed victimization of some sailors from the American ship *Baltimore*, the U. S. secretary of state obtained the authorization to use armed force to demand reparation from Chile. The *"Baltimore* incident" was used by the United States to formally warn Chile that, from that point on, it must accept North American hegemony. The government which had emerged from the civil war complied with U. S. demands, and to this day the Chilean people remember the humiliation of the *Baltimore*. They have even created a legend to symbolize the feeling of the episode, which relates how the Chilean lieutenant who was forced by U. S. authorities to lower Chile's flag committed suicide upon compliance.

Some years later, Guggenheim entered the nitrate business, and Braden went into copper. The U. S. government began to put pressure on Chile's foreign policy, both within the "Panamerican" framework (which Chile had long considered a threat to its national interests) and within its bilateral relations in South America and other parts of the world. Anaconda began its exploitation of basic mining resources, other American firms replaced the British in the principal public utilities, and ITT took over telecommunications.

Between the two world wars, Britain turned over its world leadership to the United States, and Chile changed hands. By the end of World

War II the United States was formally established as the leading imperialist power in the hemisphere. This relationship of dependency coincided with the establishment of special and exclusive military relations between the United States and the Latin American countries. In Chile's case, this took place between 1945 and 1946.

On November 13, 1970, during the first few days of the Allende government, a preliminary study of U. S.-Chile military relations was made in Chile. Part of that analysis read as follows:

> When the major hostilities of World War II ended, the United States, whose military position as a world power had replaced that of most other capitalist powers, immediately sought to establish military relations with each of the Latin American countries — thus preparing the groundwork for a new hemispheric defense system to replace the one established at the beginning of the war, which, though considered politically useful by the United States, had been proven potentially ineffective militarily.
>
> In the years following 1945–46, these plans were gradually carried out through various judicial, political, military, and financial organs; the process was accelerated by reason, or on the pretext, of the cold war, and as a result of the deteriorated economic condition of the Latin American countries, which encouraged them to sign agreements which, it appeared, would help them modernize their military equipment at reduced costs. That is how they entered into the TIAR, the Military Assistance Program, arms purchase agreements, Operation Unitas, and military training programs. Other military ties were also created in this way within the network of the OAS charter and the inter-American system, with active participation in the Inter-American Defense Council and the summit meetings of commanders in chief, for instance.
>
> Thus, to date, a complex network of military ties has been formed between our country and the United States. The various elements comprising it do not appear to be under the coordinated control of any particular organ of the Chilean executive, although theoretically the Ministry of National Defense, like its counterpart in the United States, handles every aspect of military relations between the two countries. In addition to the strictly military ties, there are also those that concern the forces of security and order (Carabineros[1] and investigative agencies) which have developed in the last few years as a result of this evolution. In principle, they would be under the Ministry of Interior's control. On the other hand, although all of the relations between the United States and Chile in these areas form an important part of our country's foreign relations, the Ministry of Foreign Affairs apparently never has had political control over them or even access to a

full knowledge of the matter, with the exception of those political
and legal matters which arise from some of the more prominent
aspects of these relations and are sometimes put in the foreground
of Chile's foreign policy — those occasions in which the Ministry
of Foreign Affairs does intervene.

In early 1971 this memorandum was supplemented by a more exhaustive study that would serve as the basis for the government's analysis of
all relations between Chile and the United States.

A revised examination of the military relations between Chile
and the United States should be undertaken. A distinction should
be made between those relations that are of a purely military character and those that are not, i.e., those which in some cases do not
come under the sphere or authority of the armed forces, but do
give insight into those bilateral relations between Chile and the
United States considered to have some military connection.

In military matters, ongoing relations between the two countries were formed within the political context of the cold war and
on a formal basis of international documents (multilateral treaties
and bilateral pacts), and through the creation of several jurisdic-
tional bodies ranging from the OAS to the Inter-American Defense
Council.

After the war, the first steps taken toward formalizing these
military relations were the bilateral Arms Lease programs, whereby
the United States gave equipment and armaments to those countries at war with the Axis nations, and established special military
relations with each of them.

Through its military strength and decisive international policy,
the United States had virtually inherited the traditional military
partnership that had existed between the Latin American countries and Germany, the other defeated nations, and a victorious
but weakened Great Britain as well. When the major hostilities
ceased, it sought to formally establish direct military relations
with the countries in this region. Accordingly, it cemented further
the political, economic, and other forms of dependence of these
countries on it and, furthermore, laid the foundation for the
hemisphere's defense system by enlisting the countries of Latin
America into its worldwide military and ideological bloc.

In 1945 special U. S. missions initiated talks in Chile to arrange
military relations between the two countries. From the outset,
U. S. objectives were clear to its diplomats and military. Proof
of this came out in confidential reports of that time which the
State Department published recently.[2] The main objectives
would be:

1. To unify, under U. S. domination, the strategy, armaments, and military doctrine in each of these countries, so as to guarantee U. S. security throughout Latin America

2. To make the United States the only source of armaments and other equipment to be used for military purposes by each of the three branches of the armed forces and the security forces of all Latin American countries, thus insuring the corresponding military and political control, as well as the consequent commercial advantages, for the U. S. armament industry

3. To create, through these channels, some kind of arms control in the region, run exclusively by the United States in accordance with its political affairs and national security so that it would be in a position to stabilize or alter the balance, as it saw fit, of the traditional military correlation between the countries in this region

4. To influence as well as to determine the quantity and distribution, in each country, of military forces in order to prepare them to support various types of American military bases at different points on the Latin American continent

5. To build up U. S. influence and political strength within each country and thereby greatly increase the capacity for action of its embassies and private interests, etc.

To what extent these objectives were successful is an important matter, but one that would require a historical analysis that is difficult to make at this time. Nevertheless, these projects were being shaped and put into effect in the years immediately following 1945–46 through various diplomatic, political, military, economic, and financial organs as the case demanded. The motive, or the pretext, of the cold war and the deteriorating economic situation of most Latin American countries at that time accelerated the process.

Later on we shall examine separately the principal multilateral and bilateral agreements, military operations and programs, and the military ties within the framework of the OAS charter and the inter-American system. We will also raise the point that these agreements, joint programs, and commitments were used by the United States in various ways as they best suited its interests at the time: first, to face the cold war; and then, to handle the so-called internal subversion and other national or international events that appeared threatening to U. S. military world security, to its political system of Latin American subjection and dependence, to its own private interests such as investments and credits in those countries, and, in general, to the role it would assume in each country, and in all of them taken as a whole. This is clear from the political-statutory turn the OAS took during the sixties, which broadened the defense of the hemisphere to cover the so-called internal subversive movements, using as an excuse the trumped-up notion that they represented a threat to the security of the hemisphere from intruders.

The relative success of the United States in this process varied from country to country and took different forms in the separate branches of the armed forces, security forces, etc. Sometimes the reaction of this or that Latin American country brought about changes in the continuity of American policy. But one can probably conclude, without going into a detailed historical investigation, that the United States was responsible for the most important of them. As changes occurred in the requirements for military security, in the political intentions of the United States toward each of the Latin American countries, and in the bilateral relations in politics and economics, corresponding variations occurred in the interpretation and implementation of agreements as well as in the function of the various units; but the role of the United States as powerful "administrator" in military affairs for each and all of them was decisive. As a matter of fact, U. S. domestic politics, as well as economic and budget problems, was sometimes the principal source of the most important variations in the military relations between the United States and Latin America. Here is an example: it was budgetary reasons (the reduction of funds of the U. S. Defense Department) along with a different concept of conventional and nuclear military security risks in South America, rather than bilateral relations, that apparently made the United States reduce the size of its military missions and implement differently the previously agreed-upon program of supplying arms and military material at the end of the sixties.

In any case, all of this led to the formation, at that time, of a very complex network of military relations between our country and the United States. This calls for a descriptive analysis of the structure of the principal military relations between Chile and the United States, while at the same time taking note of other matters that are not strictly military but do have some military connection and that may have, or will take on, a military character. By putting into practice this method of working together with the Ministry of Defense and eventually with other national sectors, some indispensable objectives may be reached:

1. To put together in one complete file all the evidence of sources of military relations existing between Chile and the United States

2. To make a thorough analysis of the real significance of these relations and to use them to formulate a program for the future

3. To be prepared to exercise central political control over this very important continuum of relations between Chile and the United States, making it conform to other aspects of our relations with that country

The preliminary conclusions (simply considering them as the basis for a future joint study) arrived at are as follows:

I. *TIAR (Inter-American Treaty for Mutual Aid).*

At first glance the military, political, and, in a sense, ideological setup of this multilateral treaty (keeping in mind its official validity) must be considered today within the historical context of the cold war during which the treaty was drawn up, and with an awareness of the circumstances that have altered that context. Thus the military demands expressed by this treaty, as well as its political and especially its ideological implications, permit some latitude of interpretation. This does not mean that, legally speaking, the TIAR is obsolete, but that it requires special attention in a future analysis of the meaning of this agreement and its system within the network of relations between the United States and Chile.

II. *PAM (Military Assistance Program).*

PAM has served as the basis for the acquisition of arms and other military equipment and for the training and exchange of military personnel between the United States and Chile. Where these matters are concerned it is the essential bilateral document between the two countries.

We can say that over the last few years, with the United States taking the initiative in its own interests and for reasons of strategy of a political and financial nature, there has been a decrease in the relevance of the procedures for military purchase, training, and so forth. This varies with respect to the three branches of the armed forces. It is more evident in the Air Force. There is a less noticeable variation in the Navy's case. It would need a special and methodical investigation to find out why and how this occurred.

Regarding the training of personnel (and here too the United States seems to have taken the initiative), the machinery that provided facilities for this, especially those of an economic nature, has to a large extent stopped operating so that there is less training now, and Chile has to foot the bill.

A special detailed study must be made of the rest of the interchanges for which PAM serves as the direct or indirect legal plan, taking into account documents that go back to this treaty but which are adapted to the various branches of the armed forces (under conditions that are not always uniform or coherent); these documents have created certain types of military relations of which we do not know the exact designation. One prior example of this kind of situation is the weather stations abandoned in the last few months. But, of course, there are numerous other examples.

In conclusion we can say that the entire legal validity of PAM now has a significance that differs from that of previous periods and that this significance depends on decisions of a political or other nature, made principally by the United States; this should draw our attention to the possibility that Chile may have more and more to say about the application of this treaty in the future.

III. *U. S. military missions in Chile*

These missions, encompassing all the branches of the United States armed forces except the Marines, have functioned officially since they were set up under separate pacts and regularly renewed. They are still active in Chile, but during the past few years, as a result of an American decision (based on budgetary and strategical reasons already mentioned), they have reduced their personnel and are now considerably smaller. This move occurred gradually, except in the case of the U. S. Naval mission. In its case the United States decided to maintain, for the time being, the necessary personnel in Chile, fulfilling an "ad hoc" arrangement that apparently has not been agreed upon or officially discussed.

The reduction in the Army and Air Force missions naturally would imply a weakening of their role as go-between in the military relations between the United States and Chile — a liaison that has been carried out, according to our information, mainly within the framework of PAM.

We should obtain exact information about (*a*) the actual number of these missions in Chile now and the significance of its reduction to the military relations anticipated within the framework of PAM, etc.; (*b*) information about these missions and future plans for them, such as eventual cutbacks of personnel, etc.; (*c*) the present situation of the Naval mission and the meaning of its variance, already mentioned, from the other two missions, as well as information about this Naval mission and future plans for it.

IV. *Chilean military missions in the United States.*

They exist in the three branches of our armed forces and were established under various agreements. Their basic role is to carry out the goals of PAM, especially with regard to purchases. This would naturally imply an important financial administration and many technical posts and functions.

From what we know these missions serve, in certain cases, as relay stations for acquisitions of a military nature in other countries, including those of Europe.

After the United States modified its system of supplying military equipment under the conditions set by PAM, the Chilean military missions in the United States began to carry out the major part of their purchases in more or less commercial terms, but with the official intervention of the U. S. Defense Department, as a result, we believe, of U. S. legal and regulatory demands. And yet, the terms of those purchases were apparently more favorable in several aspects than the strictly commercial ones. There is no doubt, however, that a special analysis would be necessary to determine whether this officially means that such purchases in the United States are made directly or indirectly through PAM.

It should be pointed out that, as far as we know, the administration of each of the three U. S. missions enjoys a high degree of autonomy with respect to the others, and deals directly and, up to a point, exclusively with the corresponding branch of the armed forces in Chile.

In the last few years the personnel and the budget of the Chilean missions have not been substantially modified.

From each of the above observations, it follows that there is a need to set down the concrete facts and information about the functioning of these three military missions in the United States.

V. *Inter-American Defense Council. Inter-American College of Defense.*

These two bodies (the second has a link of relative dependence on the first) have a rather peculiar character as organizations without official sanction in the inter-American system. Their budget is decided by the OAS, but their ties with the various sectors of the OAS suffer from a certain ambiguity, many examples of which can easily be found.

The Council representatives, who come from various branches of the armed forces of member nations of the inter-American system, take part in continuous meetings held in Washington. In almost every case these representatives are military attachés assigned to the Washington embassy of each country. According to information we have, the subjects discussed in the Council may cover aspects of a strictly military or of a political nature; thus, a good number of these debates deal with purely political questions, broached by representatives (including those from the United States) with strong ideological convictions. In this respect the traditional policy of the Chilean representatives diverges from such practice; they tend to confine the discussions strictly to military matters.

From what we understand, Chile's presence in the Council continues on terms similar to those of previous years.

As for the Council itself, we must specify (a) its standing as an institution and the limits of its function; (b) the significance of its resolutions and its various activities (especially with regard to their eventual importance and influence in the military sectors of each member nation, with any political implications they may have, since it appears that in the official, juridical, and political sense they lack jurisdiction in respect to each individual country as well as on a collective level); (c) the role the Council plays in the "ideologization" of U. S. military relations in the hemisphere; and (d) Chile's present policy toward the Council and our participation in it.

The Inter-American College of Defense, whose link to the Council has been pointed out, consists of high-ranking Latin American officers, and provides training in "professional development," unquestionably tainted with political-ideological intentions. When this body gets together for talks, conferences, etc. (in a way, this phenomenon stands out more clearly at the meetings of the Council itself), it is a center of mutual information about the role that the various representatives of the armed forces think the military institutions should play in each country and of their attitude toward questions of a political and basically economic nature. Chile's presence in the College continues under terms similar to those it has always had.

VI. *Periodic meetings of commanders in chief.*

It is not clear exactly how these meetings originated. They take place in different countries, are attended by the commanders in chief (in some cases they send a substitute representative, but this seems to be very rare), and are held separately for the three branches of the armed forces. As a matter of fact, the system of convocation is now practically automatic; the date and location of the next reunion is generally decided upon at each meeting. The agenda at these meetings vary and undoubtedly do not exclude political questions that have some connection with military problems. And ideological questions also come up. In effect, as in the case of the Inter-American Defense Council, these summit conferences serve as a collective forum for official examination and discussion of the material on the day's agenda (the end result takes the form of resolutions with a value comparable to those of the Council commented on above) and also give participants a chance to examine officially, among themselves, points of a professional nature in their respective bilateral relations. This becomes apparent when we look into the ties established by the commanders in chief of the Latin American countries and the United States in matters related to military purchases and other related subjects. This type of contact frequently leads them to consider questions of a political nature, whether or not they are international questions.

These meetings have taken place as scheduled during the past few months, and the next ones have already been planned.

One would have to make a documented analysis of the origin, nature, themes, resolutions, etc., of the meetings of the commanders in chief in order to determine — if it seems appropriate — what policy must be followed.

VII. *Operation Unitas.*

We cannot fall back on a complete set of documents in this case either. These operations obviously play a double role in the combined strategic preparations of the U. S. Navy in conjunction with the fleets of the Latin American countries, and contribute to the training of the latter.

In Chile's case, these joint naval operations are expected to continue.

On this subject, it is important for us to state precisely what we know about the original groundwork, the stated proposals, and the actual significance of these operations.

VIII. *Invitations, visits, etc., to the United States of various groups of officers (courses in high command and war training, courses for officer candidates upon graduation from their special schools, etc.) and other individual visits for officers.*

It is extremely difficult to describe the circumstances under which these trips to the United States are undertaken, their actual professional significance, and their eventual effects on other fields, for we do not think they follow a preplanned objective, but instead just happen in each individual case in an ad hoc manner corresponding to certain "traditions" in the military relations between the two countries.

For this reason we would have to conduct an examination, substantiated by documents, into the character and significance these trips have assumed in the case of Chilean officers during the last few years.

According to information we have received, it is believed that the practice or "tradition" of these visits will be stopped in the near future as a result of steps taken by, or an oversight on the

part of, the United States. This would have to be substantiated,
at the same time an analysis was made of the meaning of this
possibility.

The invitations under special pretext to titled personnel, which
have been rarer, require another chapter.

IX. *Special ties of the Cuerpos de Carabineros.*

Given the ambivalent nature of the Cuerpo de Carabineros
of Chile (a police force that is virtually a fourth branch of the
armed forces), its relations with the United States have developed
along a double channel. This became even more accentuated due
to the United States policy (following the case of Cuba and its
ideological position with respect to "subversion" in the midst of
the inter-American system) which gave a privileged position to
those armed forces of each Latin American country which could
serve the United States' anti-"subversive" ends most effectively.
Thus the Carabineros have received special treatment in the acquisition of arms (including air equipment) "for maintaining order"
and in highly "ideologized" military instruction. For instance,
commanding officers of the Carabineros have regularly taken
courses in Washington. We would do well to remember that this
particular attention given to the Carabineros, stressing their own
character as a repressive force, approximates the intense preparation in how to maintain order of a police-military type for use in
the cities, against guerrillas, etc., received by special units in the
Army and other forces on the U. S. side. This training was prefer-
ably carried out in the School of the Panama Canal Zone, and its
"professional" objective is inseparable from its ideological content.

X. *Special ties with investigative agencies.*

It is true that we lack adequate documentation on this
point, but it should be made clear that the ties between Chile's
investigative agencies and their American counterparts have become even stronger and closer in the last few years. All kinds of
contacts, justified as being of a professional nature, have gradually
led to collaboration (of which there are naturally few visible signs)
with the American intelligence services — not only with the FBI
(which would be understandable, since the latter fulfills police
functions in the fight against federal crimes in the United States),
but also with the CIA itself. In addition to these contacts we
should mention those direct invitations to come to the United
States, as well as specialized courses and the exchange of information that unquestionably exceeds the simple prevention and
pursuit of crime, and covers political areas (affecting aliens as well
as Chilean citizens and specifically aimed at "subversives"). As a

result these ties between the Chilean investigative agencies and
those of the United States call for a particularly detailed analysis,
just as the links between the Carabineros of Chile and the
American police and military services deserve careful attention.

Today, three years later, two aspects of this preliminary study strike
the eye: first, the difficulty or near-impossibility for the Chilean government of learning the exact nature and extent of these military ties — a
difficulty that existed even for the Chilean armed forces themselves due
to the complexity and variety of these relations, and in view of the fact
that they accentuated the contradictions that exist between the three
branches of these forces (or four, if we add to them the Cuerpo de Carabineros); secondly, a clear perspective that, in the case of the Navy, ties
of every order would be maintained.

After the experience of these three years, a third distinctive fact
stands out which emerged during Allende's presidency: despite the
United States' general policy of cutting down military aid loans — and
in contrast to the American financial and commercial policy of squeezing
off supplies to the Chilean government — the Pentagon's relations with
each branch of the Chilean armed forces (not only with the Navy, which
of course received special treatment) continued and, in some cases, even
multiplied. All of this took place through direct channels between the
armed forces of the two countries, sometimes countering the political
intentions of the Chilean government to diversify the sources of military supplies and to limit the privileged relationship of the Chilean armed
forces with the Pentagon.

In conclusion, the government of the United States wanted to maintain, as a basic instrument of its hegemony and independent of the fate
of private American interests in Chile, its various ties with the Chilean
armed forces, for these relations cemented Chile's dependence on the
center of the imperialist system.

2

Historically, the governing profile of American imperialism lends a great deal of attention to military control, while its private profile concentrates on economic control. These two functions make up its political supremacy.

Obtaining adequate knowledge of the characteristics and the extent of American hegemony in the military domain proved to be the first difficulty encountered by responsible Chileans. Oddly enough, they stumbled into the same obstacle in the economic field. There was a double reason for this. On the one hand, being dependent on an advanced political, economic, military, and technological system cannot help but affect a country's concrete expression of sovereignty: the organization of the state — undermining it, breaking it up, demoralizing it. On the other hand, dividing and bringing internal confusion to all the structures of the dominated country, beginning with the political and administrative, is a deliberate activity of the public and private agents of imperialism.

Thus, for example, careful calculations in 1968 made one realize that Chile's Ministry of Foreign Affairs was aware of less than half of all relations existing between Chile and the United States. It is not a question of its having political control over what it knew about in one way or another; it only had the chance to know of less than half of these activities. On the other hand, the Chilean embassy in Washington, because it was in the capital of the empire, was able at this time to know about two thirds of these bilateral arrangements. Who had full knowledge of and control over all these relations? The Americans themselves. First of all, the United States embassy in Santiago. It had the run of the entire Chilean administration, linking both the private and the public interests of the country, and reflecting public and private American interests in Chile.

By the end of the sixties, the United States knew Chile better than the Chileans themselves did.

This phenomenon, so typical of relationships of dependency, was nothing new. After the Cuban Revolution, and even more after the Bay of Pigs disaster, the U. S. government set aside large amounts of money to finance, in universities and research centers, studies with special emphasis on Latin America, beginning with the learning of the Spanish language itself (which now ranks first among foreign languages taught in the United States), and branching out into anthropology, economics, and other specialized disciplines. To give just one example, in the middle of 1964 at Michigan State University (the sadly infamous midwestern university that furnished the first American experts to go to Vietnam to "advise" Diem) there was an economic-technical unit dedicated to the study of agrarian reform in Chile, which was provided with resources superior to that of any comparable Chilean center, public or otherwise, dedicated to this question.

This explains why certain initiatives of the Chilean governments during this decade corresponded so closely to the models prepared in American academic centers and were not devoid of ties with big private interests or with the United States government. At Michigan State, before Frei won the presidential election in 1964, Charles Cumberland — an expert on Latin American questions — stated that the ideal system for solving the copper problems in Chile was a "Chileanization," similar to what had already been known elsewhere as "Mexicanizations"; that is, the purchase by the state of 51 percent of the stock of Anaconda and Kennecott. And in the circles of the Latin American Council and the Council on Foreign Relations in New York, two "establishment" centers for U. S. foreign policy and business interests, it was no secret that, in 1964, David Rockefeller's pet formula for Chilean copper was "Chileanization."

It has already been said that in regard to Chile, the United States government was particularly concerned with keeping and, if possible, strengthening its military grip, while private American interests had the economic field to themselves. This description is valid only if it is not carried to extremes. For, in matters of financing and credits (whether directed or diverted by multilateral organizations where official American influence is decisive), the government of the United States exercises its economic domination without intermediaries. In the same way, private corporations — and the case of ITT is only the most obvious and famous — apply themselves to secret intelligence and subversive activities which, in Chile's case, cover a paramilitary, if not strictly military, domain.

What was the state of economic dependence inherited by President Allende's government in 1970?

An unpublished paper on the economic relations between Chile and the United States from 1970 to 1972, dated April 1973 and written by a minister in one of President Allende's last cabinets together with an important public advisor in the Chilean Ministry of Foreign Affairs (since both are being persecuted by the junta, they will remain unnamed), had this to say on the subject:

> The sixties were characterized by the ominous emergence of visible symptoms of exhaustion in the Chilean economic system. This must be kept in mind in order to understand the government's objectives for transforming the prevailing economic structure.
>
> During the last decade the per capita income rose slowly, about 2 percent each year, though this pace slackened at the end of the sixties, falling off to 0.8 percent. The decreased pace of growth was due, in part, to an insufficient rate of investment. This oscillated between 15 and 17 percent of the national product, but dropped at the end of the decade. The rate of domestic savings was already low and diminished further, in spite of the persistent flow of foreign capital.
>
> While this growth continued its slow pace, the national income remained concentrated in the hands of a few. In 1968, for instance, 28.3 percent of the Chilean people took in 4.8 percent of the national income, while at the other extreme 2 percent of the families received 45.9 percent.[1] These facts explain the progressive growth of those social groups which tested the viability of the economic system and its ability to respond to the aspirations of the swelling population. As a result of this slow growth the fight for higher and more evenly distributed income gradually gained momentum. Organized labor and the lasting power and significance of the large parties on the left provided an outlet for these expectations, which had grown out of the obvious inadequacy and injustice of the economic structure and power in the country.
>
> These symptoms of the Chilean economy reflected two decisive

structural trends: an important concentration of the means of production, and significant foreign control of the economy as a result of both the property holdings of strategic companies and the foreign debt.

Up until 1965 a system dominated by the "latifundium" prevailed in the country's agricultural sector, with most of the land in the hands of a few owners. Production practically was kept at a standstill, and the peasant class often found itself relegated to the margin of the market. There was no social or cultural organization to protect this class, and it was politically controlled by the big landowners. After 1965 agrarian reform was started; by 1970 part of the "latifundia" had been expropriated, and land distribution had been organized.

The concentration of property was especially notorious in industry, but it also extended to the banking system. The groups in control of these activities were in a position to drain off a high proportion of the credit and to manipulate the better part of the financial resources. From this economic advantage, it was an easy step to political control.

In short, these facts gradually made it clear that the economic system then in effect was exhausted and could not respond to the needs of the country's vast majority.

The second half of the sixties witnessed an attempt to change the course of the economy through partial reforms that would modernize existing structures, as in the case of the agrarian reform. These conciliatory changes were carried out in line with American interests. Negotiations took place, and the state purchased interests in foreign companies, formed jointly-owned mixed companies, and received an important flow of foreign credits and capital investments.

This was an attempt to modernize, not to transform, these structures. Consequently, the applied policies increased the national debt even more, and eventually led to foreign infiltration into company ownership.

If one looks carefully at Chile's economic ties with the United States, one will notice that at the end of the last decade Chile's economy was hardly autonomous. Its main characteristics were heavy external debts, a high proportion of exports controlled from outside the country, a rapid industrial denationalization, and a very inadequate technological capacity.

The tendency to accumulate debts no matter what economic policy was applied by various administrations made it clear that the country's economic structure could not support its own expansion. In 1960 the foreign debt was $598 million. It had reached $1.8 billion by the mid-sixties, and was up to $3 billion by 1970.[2]

As a result Chile ended up with one of the highest per capita debts in the world.

Increasing indebtedness is one of the characteristics of an economy that is not self-sufficient. Such an economic system cannot survive without foreign backing. Thus, the national debt becomes an instrument to control local economies and to make them permanently dependent on foreign interests.

In addition, the control of exports by foreign corporations further weakened the economy. Copper represented the bulk of national exports, reaching 77 percent of the total in 1970. In that year the big mines, mostly controlled by the United States, produced 80 percent of the copper and consequently 60 percent of total exports. Moreover, foreign interests controlled other important exports, such as nitrate and iron.

It should be pointed out that in 1965 the government started a program for the formation of jointly-owned mixed companies, which it called the "Chileanization" of copper. The state bought 51 percent of the shares of one of the large mines (Kennecott) and 25 percent of the other (Anaconda). Both purchases were made by mutual consent and without any kind of conflict with the companies concerned. This agreement was very beneficial for the American firms, which saw large profits. As a result, strong pressures were put on the Chilean government to force it to change this policy. This happened in 1969 when the government renegotiated with Anaconda and opened the way for nationalization. Nevertheless, the policy of mutual agreement prevailed once more, and the state's share of the property rose from 25 percent to 51 percent, with an option to buy after 1973.

These feeble attempts to recover a part of the country's natural wealth were reduced to nothing by the steadily growing U. S. penetration into other industries. The most modern enterprises were gradually taken over by foreign firms and were often turned into monopolies, due to the weakness of the Chilean market. Foreign companies obtained a strong foothold in the chemical and automobile industries and in capital and consumer goods. Moreover, the rapid growth of these industries encouraged the process of denationalization.

This phenomenon went hand in hand with the growth of technological dependence. The technology used was brought in from abroad, generally without either selective judgment or an eye to its compatibility with national objectives. Very rarely were innovations made in the country. It was invariably more convenient and cheaper, at going market prices, to import technology. More than half the license fees went to the United States.

In addition, a remarkable proportion of productive capacity

depended on American capital. Maintenance of equipment required spare parts from the United States; they generally could not be found elsewhere.

At the same time, an influx of short- and long-term financing and of capital goods had begun which, combined with the volume of trade with the United States and the presence in Chile of firms from that country, gave this system of economic dependence the chance to work.

Finally, in the sixties, the capitalist economies saw the multinational companies develop at a vigorous pace. With their expansion limited by the slow growth of their domestic market, the American companies were the first to branch out into the rest of the world in order to keep up their high rate of growth. Feeling the pressure from American competitors in their own markets, major European and Japanese enterprises felt driven to invest abroad in order to maintain their relative importance. The struggle for control of the international market got tougher, and Latin America became one of its battlegrounds, especially in the industrial sector. That is why ITT's aggressive role in Chile is so significant; it shows how determined U. S. capital was to keep Latin America as a *terra nostra* of the United States.

In sum, the United States had at its disposal a number of devices that allowed it, directly or indirectly, to have decisive influence in the making and conducting of Chile's economic policy, and in the overall running of its economic system.

To illustrate the extent of Chile's economic dependence on the United States when the Popular Unity government came into power, it will be useful to show how certain private interests played a decisive role in the United States' intervention.

First of all, of course, there is ITT. This international consortium, or multinational "conglomerate," had been developing and shifting its areas of interest in Chile for many years. Not satisfied with its monopoly on telephonic and other communications, as well as on the property for installations in Chile, it poured capital into other businesses, such as hotel chains. But the strange thing about ITT, pointed out by Anthony Sampson in his book *The Sovereign State of ITT* (1973), is that in 1970 this consortium was operating telephone systems — its initial function and supposedly the focus of its activities — in only three places: Puerto Rico, where Colonel Behn, ITT's founder, had launched his business; the Virgin Islands; and the Republic of Chile. We can get an idea of the latitude ITT obtained when we consider the limited sovereignty enjoyed by the first two. Chile was the most important by far. The company

assessed its interests there at $150 million, employing six thousand
workers. From the time it was purchased from the British in 1930, and
since the original concession called for payments in gold, the operation
had earned considerable revenues and required little investment. The
expansion of the telephone network in the sixties brought in new and
very profitable business. Such was the case in 1966, for instance, when
ITT's proposals were accepted over those of the Swedish company, Erics-
son. This transaction was denounced in France and Sweden and is pointed out in Sampson's book. In short, not only did ITT possess considerable
and highly profitable economic interests in Chile — something unique,
in our day, for this kind of service — but, naturally, it assumed the role
of coordinator of all private U. S. interests. Even if its investments and
earnings in Chile were smaller than those of other firms, like Anaconda
and Kennecott, the worldwide nature of its operations gave it the advantage of political insight into the policies of the United States, both domestic and foreign, which the other companies could not hope to have.
Anaconda and Kennecott belonged to the old imperial order, while
ITT — rejecting as outmoded those capitalist activities that relied on raw
materials — represented the spearhead, in Chile, of the new imperialism.

A few words on Anaconda and Kennecott. Trying to discover the
actual value of their interests in Chile was like trying to see in the dark.
They had been there so long, and — as the old saying goes — they
pulled the treasure from the earth, took it home, and left us the hole.
As a matter of fact, the hole of Kennecott's El Teniente is the largest
underground copper mine, and Anaconda's operation at Chuquicamata
is the largest open-pit copper mine in the world. But for Chileans, including those in the government and in Congress who, in early 1971,
discussed and later unanimously approved the nationalization of copper,
the price of those holes and their installations — if a value can be put
on such riches and such spoils — has always been a total mystery. An
economic mystery? No, a political mystery. In any case, we have only
to remember what President Allende so often said: the profits taken
out of Chile by Anaconda and Kennecott are at least equivalent to the
total capital accumulated by Chile since it got started in 1541. Those
two companies have wrested an entire Chile from Chile in a very short
period of time — a whole Chile lost to the Chileans forever. Because of
imperialism Chile is today only half the country it should be. . . .

For many years Anaconda and Kennecott had been prepared for
nationalization, should it come. For instance, they obtained an exor-
bitant scope of benefits thanks to the *Nuevo Trato* (New Treaty) of

1955, and even more after the Chileanizations of 1965-69. Denounced in 1969 by Senator Narciso Irureta, a Christian Democrat, and amply documented in 1970 and 1971 by Luis Maira, another Christian Democrat (to cite testimony from ex-President Frei's party), these gains provoked a real political and economic scandal. In New York well-known experts on Latin American affairs were already anticipating the inevitable nationalization of Chilean copper exploited by the Americans.

One of these experts was David Bronheim, former coordinator of the Alliance for Progress, a member of the Latin American Council, and a very close friend of David and Nelson Rockefeller. (He accompanied Nelson Rockefeller on his difficult 1969 tour of Latin America, which had been arranged by Nixon and which resulted in the important *Rockefeller Report on the Quality of Life in the Americas.* This report almost overtly advocates, as a future prospect, military regimes for the continent.) Bronheim declared on June 12, 1970, in a closed meeting devoted to the question of "Copper and Politics in the United States, Africa, and South America," before an audience made up of the principal U. S. foreign investors and the economic advisers of the Nixon administration (such as Hendrik Houthakker), that there was no doubt in his mind that Chile would nationalize copper soon — that is, right after the presidential elections that year — for it already had the means, including technical ones, to do it.

In spite of this, or perhaps because of it, neither Anaconda nor Kennecott nor the U. S. government was prepared to accept the nationalization. Let us overlook the international repercussions of a nationalization that is legally and politically foolproof; let us not consider the fact that we are dealing with copper, strategically important both to industry and to the military; let us even forget that Chile is one of the largest producer-exporters of copper in the world, and that a joint political decision with Zambia and Zaire could lead to control of this product in the world market. Over and above this, the actual value of U. S. mines and operations extracting Chilean copper, no matter how difficult to ascertain, exceeded — according to general estimates — the value of any U. S. property nationalized anywhere in the world in the last ten years. Experts say that the only nationalization comparable to this was that of the Suez Canal, which definitely did not extend to the stocks of the Societé Financière du Canal, and which permitted important capitalist interests to claim some indemnifications. Without going that far, it is obvious that the much bruited nationalizations of the sixties were far less important than that of Chilean copper. On the other hand, Mossadegh's nationalization

of Iranian oil makes a good comparison. We know what happened to
Mossadegh and the part the United States and its secret intelligence
played in Iran.

During his tour of Latin America in 1965, Robert Kennedy stayed in
Santiago for a few days and met with a group of Chilean intellectuals.
Richard Goodwin accompanied him. Dr. Vicente Sánchez (today in
Geneva) and Dr. Ignacio Matte (in Rome) were among those intellectuals.
At this meeting, which was not publicized, the second Kennedy brother
spoke of "American imperialism" — in quotes — and said that Latin
American intellectuals and politicians of the Left were quite mistaken
in believing that the U. S. government identified itself with the private
interests of investors operating in their countries; most of those American companies lacked economic importance and political strength in
the United States and were in no condition to pressure their government.
Several Chileans responded with outrage: first, speaking only of Chile,
Anaconda and Kennecott were not small in the United States and, what
is more, were giants in Chile; secondly, one of those present had witnessed how, in 1954 when negotiations with these companies on the
subject of the *Nuevo Trato* were about to begin, the assistant secretary
of state for Latin America, Henry Holland, representing the United
States at a meeting with the Chilean minister of mines, had stressed the
need for Anaconda and Kennecott to receive the best possible treatment;
finally, that this was just one case among many in which the U. S.
government intervened on behalf of private American interests in Chile.
(One had only to read the official documents the State Department was
publishing, twenty-five years late.)

Robert Kennedy listened through to the end. "If one president of
the United States, whom I don't want to name, had only lived longer . . ."
His voice broke off sadly.

Eight years later, with hundreds of other similar experiences, we could
finish the sentence: If that president had lived, none of this would have
changed. There is no hope of change in the imperialist system. During
the past eight years Anaconda and Kennecott, ITT and the U. S. government have acted in each other's interests, together, hand in hand.
Imperialism sticks together; it's a system.

3

Project Camelot, a plan set up by the U. S. Defense Department to study potential subversion at all levels in a developing country, was financed with more money than any other investigation in the history of the social sciences. They attempted to try it out on Chile in 1965. Disclosures by Alvaro Bunster, who at that time was general secretary of the University of Chile and later on became President Allende's ambassador in London until the coup, provoked its failure and caused a scandal in the international community of sociologists, which still considers the project to be a classic illustration of political intervention. It was a magnificent example of how the U. S. government uses the social sciences for subversive ends. It is studied in social science classes in Europe and America, for it poses the problem of professional ethics, morality, and political conviction. Several case studies on it have appeared during the last few years; for instance, *Project Camelot: Cancelled.* (Similarly, the "Secret Memos from ITT" on the series of plots organized by this multinational company, in conjunction with the government in Washington, to stop Salvador Allende from gaining power and later to overthrow him are studied in a number of foreign services because they provide a "test case" of the close relations existing between private groups and the U. S. government and of the characteristics, style, hook-up, and contradictions of this partnership. It is quite possible that the coup of 1973 will also serve as a classic example of U. S. involvement in a *coup d'etat*, and that its technique and history will be studied. What a poor consolation for those Chileans who are still fighting and dying.)

Never had a sociological investigation as ambitious as Project Camelot been conceived: to study the entire society of a country in order to measure its political capacity for revolution, to calculate its social aggressiveness, and to find out how strong it would be under repression. Spying on a whole country. The political objectives could be seen clearly through the scientific guise. The Pentagon was the instigator, under cover of a contract with the American University in Washington, D.C. Until the project was publicly revealed, the American ambassador in Chile, Ralph Dungan, had not been informed of its existence. The State Department declared that it had not received any information on the subject. Dungan, who had worked with John Kennedy, invoked the official directive, passed after the disaster of the Bay of Pigs, that intelligence operations on such a wide scale required authorization at the highest policy level. He also claimed his prerogatives as the U. S. ambassador to Chile. By order of the president, the Pentagon dropped the project in record time.

But, in essence, the project was carried out. Not on the scale conceived for it in 1965. Nor were legions of sociologists deployed, as had been the case in South Vietnam. The threat of scandal would not permit it. Instead it was done a little at a time, prudently, modestly, with the help of traditional means: public and private agencies in Chile, businessmen, nonprofit organizations, the Peace Corps (yes, the Peace Corps, so idealistic, has provided experts on Latin American affairs for the U. S. government and for private U. S. concerns there), graduate students working on their doctoral dissertations, and so forth.

It is not easy to determine just how the United States gradually put together, by these means, the information the Pentagon sought with Project Camelot. But an important, little-known work, presented in 1967 as a doctoral dissertation in sociology at the University of California in Los Angeles, shows to what extent the possible disintegration of Chilean society had been measured. This study is entitled *Military Culture and Organizational Decline: A Study of the Chilean Army.*[1] Its author, Roy Hansen, a researcher for the Rand Corporation in 1961-62, was a consultant for the same company from 1962 to 1965, and made three trips to Chile in 1964-65. His analysis was based on questionnaires put to Chilean citizens (two hundred civilians interviewed, thirty-eight retired generals, and an undetermined number of the military still on active duty, chosen from among those taking courses at the Academy of War and at the polytechnical school). Among the questions asked the civilians were these:

> "Under what circumstances, if there are any, do you believe that the military could take over the government?"

"Under what circumstances would you personally support or reject a military attempt to take control of the government?"

"What do you believe are the main reasons why the Army has not been involved in any major attempts at controlling the government during the last twenty-five or thirty years?"

Among the questions asked the thirty-eight retired generals were the following:

"While you were in the Army, did you consider yourself as a Rightist, somewhat Rightist, somewhat Leftist, or as a Leftist?"

"In general, did you especially sympathize with any political party?"

"A questionnaire given a sample of the Chilean population shows a great faith of the civilians in that the military would defend the Constitution if it were violated. Specifically, under what circumstances do you believe that the military ought to act in this matter?"

"Following, I will read to you some opinions that have been given upon the military. For each proposition, please indicate to me if you agree strongly, agree a little, disagree a little, or disagree strongly with them. You may explain your opinion if you think it necessary: . . . (h) In a country that needs and is undergoing a rapid economic and social change, democracy is a luxury that often can't be afforded since it does not have the strength necessary to advance the required transformation."

The questionnaires for civilians and retired generals were preceded by a note assuring them of anonymity:

"Due to their purely scientific character the answers will be strictly confidential. They will be subjected to a process of statistical analysis that will make it impossible to identify the authors of these opinions."

And yet, on the questionnaire answered by the officers still on active duty, the most important of these groups, while confidentiality was assured and the officers were not required to sign their names, each form requested the following information:

(a) Rank; (b) Arm of Service; (c) Unit or School now attached to; (d) Place of birth; (e) Occupation of your father; (f) Occupation of father-in-law; (g) Relatives in Armed Forces or Carabineros:

Type of relationship, rank, branch; (h) Education (in number of
years): High School, University; Military School; Academy of
War; Academy Polytechnical; Foreign Military Schools; (i) Rank
in class of Military School.

Among the questions asked those officers whose rank in 1964-65 was
captain and up, as high as lieutenant colonel, since they were attending
military command training courses (and who were therefore already
colonels or even generals at the time of the coup), were these:

"If you had to choose between the following categories, in
which of them would you place yourself politically at the present
time? Please comment on the source of your decision and the
significance that you attribute to the concept pointed out:
(a) Rightist; (b) Somewhat rightist; (c) Somewhat leftist; (d) Leftist."
"In your military career, what have been the principal sources
of satisfaction for you?"
"Likewise, what have been the principal sources of dissatisfaction for you?"

After a question just like the one asked the retired generals about the
circumstances in which the military must act in order to defend the
Constitution if it were violated, the questionnaire to the officers on
active duty stressed:

"Following you will find some opinions that have been expressed
about the military. For each proposition please indicate if you
agree strongly, agree a little, disagree a little, or disagree strongly
with them: . . . (e) The military is necessary for the country even
if there is no war in order to act as a guardian of the Constitution
in case a government would try to violate it."

Several conclusions in Hansen's study are revealing. Most of them are in
Chapter 4, "Public Orientations toward the Military: Part II — Involvement in Politics." It says there:

"Despite Chile's tradition of democratic stability and the recent
history of nonintervention by their military institutions, public
opinion still accepted the military as a guardian of the Constitution.
. . . Societal consensus on the legitimacy and importance of this
role was, in fact, as great or greater than that of its more conventional military functions . . . .
Military autonomy was likewise a key factor in their role as a

check upon arbitrary authority or governmental ineffectiveness.
Chile's history of democratic stability has been achieved in spite of
numerous sources of potential conflict in the socio-economic and
political structure of the society. Unresolved conflicts smoldered
beneath the surface of political stability, erupting spasmodically
into demonstrations, riots, strikes, and radical political movements.
Perception of a need for military intervention may have reflected
both the fundamental nature of the issues involved and an underlying lack of confidence in the political institutions of the
society . . . .
    . . . Inability of the government to maintain internal order or
avoid the threat of civil war legitimized military intervention . . . .
    The perceived need of the public for a semi-autonomous mili-
tary establishment capable of acting as a check upon and/or
alternative to the government appeared to derive from the public's underlying distrust of civilian political and administrative
institutions.

Naturally, it is easy to justify this work as an impartial social analysis, an
academic work. But its preparation and its text involve a mass of information no science has the right to root out of a people. This information
pertains to the basic political convictions of a sovereign country. The
data gathered by the Rand Corporation's consultant have been used by
the United States against Chile.

The fact that Project Camelot had been a Pentagon operation sheds
light on United States policy toward Chile and other Latin American
countries, and the policy still continues. Since the mid-sixties, the
Defense Intelligence Agency has held most of the responsibility for
gathering intelligence on Chile. The CIA's errors in Cuba persuaded the
Kennedy administration to relieve it of many operations that were then
handed over to the Pentagon.

The United States' strong interest in the Chilean military came to
light in 1969. In October of that year a military uprising took place in
Chile for the first time in decades — the revolt of the Tacna regiment
in Santiago. This regiment was led by General Roberto Viaux, who,
ITT documents show, in October 1970 was preparing a "preventive" coup
against Allende and receiving advice directly from the United States.
"It is a fact that word passed to Viaux from Washington to hold back
last week. It was felt that he was not adequately prepared, his timing
was off, and he should 'cool it' for a later, unspecified date. Emissaries
pointed out to him that if he moved prematurely and lost, his defeat
would be tantamount to a 'Bay of Pigs in Chile.' As a part of the per-

suasion to delay, Viaux was given oral assurances he would receive
material assistance and support from the U.S. and others for a later
maneuver." It says so in the memorandum of October 16, 1970, dic-
tated by telephone from H. Hendrix in San Juan to ITT's Vice President
Gerrity.

But even before Viaux's Tacna venture, significant events had
occurred. In April 1969, the ministers of foreign affairs of all the Latin
American countries met in Chile and agreed, for the first time in their
history, to adopt a common stand before the United States regarding
commercial and financial matters. The document approved by them
was called the *Consenso de Viña del Mar* (the Viña del Mar Agreement),
and the Chilean foreign minister, Gabriel Valdés, was unanimously
authorized to present it personally to President Nixon.

Nixon did not want to grant Valdés an interview. But by June he
could no longer put him off. The meeting took place on June 11, 1969.
At this incredible event Valdés, accompanied by Domingo Santa María
(his ambassador), Ramón Huidobro (Allende's ambassador in Buenos
Aires until the coup), and Armando Uribe (later ambassador in Peking
until the coup) confronted President Nixon in the cabinet room of the
White House. Secretary of State William Rogers and Henry Kissinger
were next to Nixon. All the Latin American ambassadors to the White
House encircled them.

Gabriel Valdés did not present the document with a few words of
routine introduction. He spoke of the impossibility of dealing with the
United States within the regular framework of inter-American relations;
the differences in power were too great. In return for each dollar it
invested in America, the United States invariably took away five. Nixon
was caught off guard. (So were some of the Latin American ambassadors.) Masking his irritation, Nixon heard Valdés out, and then pulled
himself together, lowering his eyelids, becoming impenetrable, withdrawn. Kissinger frowned.

Those who know Washington say that, as far as anyone could recall,
no president of the United States had ever looked so affronted. This
may be true, at least in Nixon's case, with the exception of the day he
was bombarded with tomatoes in Caracas. (He recalled this experience
in his answer to Valdés.)

The fact is that neither Valdés's speech, nor Nixon's reply, nor the
solemn handing over of the Latin American *Consenso*, appears to
have been recorded by the United States. For the Nixon administration this historic event simply had not occurred.

What did Nixon say? Today, his words are important in order to understand recent events in Chile. A private document of that time, based on the notes of Armando Uribe, reports them.

When Valdés had delivered his statement and the document to President Nixon, the latter made the following improvised speech[2]:

>I want to thank Minister Valdés for his frankness and sincerity. I too want to examine the present state of inter-American relations, but I also want to do it through the eyes of Latin America. As I examine these relations, I want us to stand on the same level, the United States and Latin America, not one looking down on the other and the other looking up. Getting together like this is very important for us. We must respect the right of other nations to choose their own way, and we must not interfere with decisions that are theirs to make.
>
>However, I have doubts about the possibility of a consensus in Latin America. Coming to an agreement is a hard thing to do and I am not sure that the conditions for political agreement in Latin America are ripe today.
>
>Your mission, Minister Valdés, is very important, and I have listened very carefully to what you have told me. The points agreed on at the meeting in Viña del Mar interest me very much. I am pleased that you have come because now we have a chance to discuss the affairs of the hemisphere in an open and direct manner.
>
>I fully agree with all the principles set down by the president of CECLA.[3] I don't object in any way to the various points you have raised. This is a good presentation of the problems that face us. The difficulty lies in finding solutions and the means needed to solve those problems.
>
>I would like to take up four points.
>
>The first is private investment. I agree that private investment should not be considered aid. It is not aid. It's business and profits are its rewards. But private investment does have a very important part to play in any country's development. This has been the case in my own country. And the same thing goes for other countries, because the examples of success in foreign aid are precisely those in which such aid has laid the groundwork for a massive inflow of private investment. Such is the case in the Republics of Korea, Taiwan, South Vietnam, and the Philippines. Moreover, even when governments want to put as much capital as possible into financial assistance to other countries, their resources are always limited. On the other hand, private resources multiply easily if they are given sufficient guarantees. Private capital which can be invested in Latin America — not only capital from the United States but also from other countries — increases

the possibilities of government cooperation and renders it more effective.

Now I'd like to bring up a very controversial issue: Governor Rockefeller's visits to Latin America. I want to make it very clear that I don't consider the demonstrations during those visits as hostile acts against the governor or against the United States, nor do I consider them an expression of the majority feeling in those countries. During my own trip through Latin America I got some rough treatment too, but I realized that it didn't reflect the feeling of the people, and I did not consider it an offense against me personally or against the United States, but simply the work of certain restless minority groups. It did not represent the majority of the people's feelings or those of the governments of Latin America at that time, and it doesn't represent them now. There are violent people everywhere. You come from a democratic country and you know about these things. You are also a politician. I told myself then that not everybody in Latin America is anti-American. The same thing happened to Nelson Rockefeller, but he is also a politician and knows that such demonstrations aren't against the United States or against him. The fact is, such actions can give some people in this country a false impression of Latin America. Still, we have to admit that there are signs of restlessness all over the world, and the United States is also having its strong share of troubles in the universities.

We have to find new ways of communication between the United States and Latin America. That's why CECLA is important. I feel optimistic about the prospect of long-term economic development in Latin America. I am impressed by the generosity, the capacity for work, and the desire for progress in Latin America. It has enormous human, as well as natural, resources. Its people, its lands, have an extraordinary potential that can be put to very fruitful use.

I realize that it can be a potential volcano, filled with disparate forces and tensions, but volcanic lands are the richest — those made up of volcanic ashes: when they cease to erupt, and the land cools, they can be worked very successfully. I know this because I have seen it in American territory, in Hawaii.

The last thing I want to say is that we live in times of revolution and, consequently, we have to face many problems. But in the end, we are preparing a society such as the world has never seen. The United States can set this goal for itself, because it has created within its own borders a society worthy of envy. This enables us to do what we are actually doing in all fields.

We have to work together at this task. We want to work with you. While we may see some things differently, we have the same objectives and accept the same principles. It would have been easier for us to go on with the existing programs, but we have decided to reexamine U. S. policy in order to reach our common objectives. There is one thing you must not doubt: we are with you.

It is only now, more than four years after that embarrassing improvisation, so typical of Nixon's style, so avid and filled with undeclared loathing, that one gets the full meaning of the most banal passage in the speech (who would ever have thought of it?): the metaphor about Latin America as a volcano of revolutions whose eruption the United States awaits because it knows — having seen the same thing on American territory, in *Hawaii* — that once the lava cools and the ashes settle, mixing into the earth, everything will be ready and just right for the reaping.

You will say that this is being a little too subtle, but Mr. Nixon and Dr. Kissinger are complicated beings. They act through allusions, they give warning in soft tones, hedging with metaphors.

After the revolution (there has to be one, there is a will like a machine behind all this) the repression will crush us. Then the money will have its chance again.

In 1969 Nixon was not yet quite at home in the presidential role. With Kissinger at his side, he learned self-control and gained self-confidence. Shades of Woodrow Wilson and Colonel House! Kissinger has the professor's self-assurance. He is not a man of large social or official gatherings.

Around the time of this meeting of Valdés and Nixon, Dr. Kissinger visited the Chilean embassy. He did not speak about Chile or South America. He said, "I am not interested in, nor do I know anything about, the southern portion of the world from the Pyrenees on down." Tapping his fingers on the table, he seemed distracted. But he wasn't missing a word. Everybody knows that the tap of fingers on wood interferes with any secret tape recording of a conversation. Kissinger's words were not meant to be taped. "I'm not losing any sleep over Berlin . . . . The United States entered the war in Vietnam not only without knowing anything about Vietnam, but because it didn't know anything about Vietnam."

Almost a year later, with the Chilean presidential campaign in full swing, Kissinger returned to the embassy. His interest in Chile had grown; he said that he would like to go there, but feared that his trip would be interpreted wrongly. He asked about the snow and about the whales in the Pacific; he made up a clever geographical joke about the danger of sliding from the Chilean Andes down into a whale's gaping

mouth. He wanted to know about the elections. What was the difference between Allende's program and Tomic's? And, if there were no
great differences, why were there two candidates? And why, after all,
were there three, and not two? (Alessandri was the third candidate.)
Crafty, inscrutable Kissinger . . .

Midway in 1969 the Frei government, following the suggestion of
members of its party, and as a result of negotiations with the copper
companies conducted by a minister and three experts, decided to pro-
ceed with the "promised nationalization." This plan was attacked by
the Christian Democratic deputy, Luis Maira, who criticized it point by
point as a damaging step for Chile,[4] and by another Catholic, Eduardo
Novoa.[5]

In the second half of 1969, National Educational Television prepared
an extensive report on U. S. military and economic interventions throughout the world, entitled "Who Invited Us?" The program could not be
shown in the United States. It was considered contrary to national interests. In this report, Senator Karl Mundt, distinguished member of
the U. S. Senate Committee on Foreign Relations, gave his views on a
socialist Chile:

> Well, we'd be hurt in the first case because we have a lot of
> American interests in Chile. They would immediately appropriate
> them, they wouldn't compensate the owners, the American owners,
> for them. They would discontinue wherever they could trading
> with the United States, in favor of trading with the Communist
> bloc. They would do what Communists always do, expanding
> organization, aggressive in nature, imperialistic in design. They
> would immediately start working on their Latin American neigh-
> bors, so we would be in jeopardy with our relationships with
> Latin America, just as Cuba, having a Communist government,
> sends infiltrators constantly into other Latin American areas try-
> ing to overthrow the government and set up a Communist camp.
> And you wouldn't want a government down there run by a Com-
> munist, because this would be terrifying. It would probably mean
> that we would indeed have to become isolationist and arm our-
> selves, and base ourselves. And how you would then avert an
> atomic attack, and eventually a holocaust, I just wouldn't be able
> to imagine.

On the Sunday before the Tacna uprising in Santiago, at the end of
October 1969, Agustín Edwards — the most powerful magnate in
Chile, heir to the newspaper chain of *El Mercurio* and then president

of the Inter-American Press Society (Sociedad Interamericana de Prensa, or SIP) — appeared in Washington, D.C. He supposedly went there for the annual meeting of SIP, which is a center of propaganda and information for allied Latin and North American interests, a stock market for political-economic influences in the hemisphere. However, the SIP meeting was not scheduled to start until several days later. Edwards seemed very preoccupied. He was accompanied by several dignitaries, outstanding among them Cubillos, a retired naval officer. What was going on? Edwards was incoherent. He spoke in broken words, saying that "they" were ready to make their move, "they" were not waiting any longer, that the government was obviously in the know, that this was a very critical moment — but, "As you can see, I'm not in Santiago now. I have my reasons for coming here."

It was impossible to make head or tail of what he was saying then. A few days later General Roberto Viaux's "Tacnazo" hit the news, and Edwards's disconnected words began to make sense. Agustín Edwards had known all about this coup that was to take place before the election. What he didn't know, perhaps, was that this coup would fizzle out.

Edwards made use of his stay in Washington to meet more than once at the home of one of the military attachés of the embassy, with the Chilean officers who were in closest contact with their American colleagues. At least on one occasion, several of these colleagues were also present, asked questions and received answers about Chilean politics and the coming presidential elections. Captain Arturo Troncoso played an active part in this meeting as the trusted go-between for the American officers.[6] Edwards also used his visit to work his way into a big American company, in case events in Chile should endanger his business interests in that country. He ate with Nixon, probably talked with Kissinger, and supplied his American friends with inside information on Chile. A year later, when Allende was elected, Agustín Edwards became one of the vice presidents of Pepsi-Cola.

On December 31, 1969, Joseph J. Jova, U. S. ambassador to the OAS (based in Washington), and chargé d'affaires in Chile in 1964, privately revealed his views about the future relations between the United States and Chile. Not only had he been politically active and effective in the presidential elections in 1964 (he had helped persuade the Chilean Right to support Eduardo Frei), but he had even been accused of direct (though discreet) intervention in other phases of Chile's domestic political affairs, although this could not be definitely proved. He was obviously looking beyond the Frei government to the 1970 elections.

An Account of a Meeting
between Joseph Jova and Armando Uribe

(December 31, 1969)

Jova explained what he thought should be the "style" of diplomatic, political, and economic relations between the United States and Chile in the coming years. He said that perhaps the United States' chief error was that it had been too soft, and had not made its own interests felt strongly enough; that the United States had acted "like someone hitting a mattress with a pillow, when he should have used a hammer and an anvil. Even if sparks flew in the process, our mutual relations and interests would have been better served, without leaving any room for misunderstanding." Then he announced, in words that were not very clear, a future of bilateral relations in which the United States would take a harder and more rigid line than before, since the soft line in its relations with Chile had not paid off. There was no trace of a threat in his voice, not the slightest, but perhaps that was because Jova was such a versatile and shrewd diplomat. What he said is almost identical to what was expressed in a pompous and offensive way by Korry, the U. S. ambassador in Santiago. It is clear that relations between the United States and Chile will get tougher, more down-to-earth, stripped of all sympathetic elements, strictly businesslike and inflexible. Finally, according to Jova, the new international policy defined by Kissinger means that certain South American countries will be excluded from the framework of direct U. S. interests unless it turns out (by some instinctive reaction, Jova emphasized) that one of these countries becomes a real threat to the basic interests of the United States. In conclusion, Jova wondered out loud whether it would have been better if, in the past, the Marines had appeared ready to intervene in Chile. Yes, I answered, that would definitely have made all the Chilean people band together, and you would have been faced with a solid bloc.

It was the beginning of 1970. Following Chilean law, the presidential elections were to be held September 4. ITT sized up the situation and made its forecasts. Its president, Harold Geneen, stuck by the company's "motto": Above all, no surprises! Dr. Kissinger was starting to take a real interest in Chile. At the Pentagon, preparations were underway for a contingency plan for intervention in Chile.

4

Following the attempted coup by Roberto Viaux and his "Tacna" regiment in Santiago in 1969, Eduardo Frei's government was forced to reexamine the military situation. It included figures like Undersecretary Patricio Silva Garín, a former military doctor, who played an important part in the negotiations — partly economic and partly administrative — which resulted in the rebels' capitulation. As a matter of fact, the Christian Democratic administration, like the majority of its predecessors since the middle of the 1930s, did not have a well-defined policy toward the armed forces, confident that after their frustrated attempts to run the country several times between 1924 and 1932 the armed forces had resigned themselves to a "professional role," totally subordinate to the civil government. Episodes like the dispute between the branches of the armed forces about the Navy's right to have its own air force (which was resolved in the Navy's favor when its commander-in-chief, Admiral Neumann, resigned in order to stress the importance he placed on the question) seemed to confirm the general belief that while the services might be at odds among themselves, they were loyal to the law.

In his analysis at the end of his ill-starred trip to Latin America (when Chile, as well as other countries, had told him it would not be wise to visit there), Rockefeller predicted that the number of military regimes on the continent would inevitably grow. His satisfaction could be read between the lines. Lulled into security by forty years of peace without military interference, Chile was impressed neither by Rockefeller's

statement nor by a report presented a few months later at the meeting
of the IDB[1] in Uruguay by Paul Prebisch, an Argentinian expert on
Latin American development and a leader of CEPAL and ECOSOL.[2]
Prebisch saw only two solutions for the development of the region: to
reach and to maintain a growth rate of 8 percent. This could be done
either through freely accepted social cooperation or through imposed
discipline. According to Prebisch, freely accepted cooperation would
be something unprecedented, and the other could only be imposed by a
totalitarian government. He may not have been trying to justify armed
dictatorship, but his work, which was formulated at the headquarters of
IDB in Washington, was a warning signal; at the same time it showed
that there was a sound basis for the spread of military regimes in Latin
America. The rise to power of a military government in Peru was
viewed with interest in Chile, but was considered hardly relevant to its
own situation.

Yet, many articles that spoke of a new era of military power in Latin
America were beginning to appear in American magazines specializing
in political science and international politics. Even a Chilean, Claudio
Veliz, published one of these articles in New York's *Foreign Affairs*.

In the second half of the sixties, the Chilean armed forces showed a
growing interest in having a say in the running of the government. But
an internal document written by the military, defining their idea of the
"national objective," received little attention. Hansen's thesis of
"organizational decline" and its possible consequences was ignored.
There was a general feeling, justifiable perhaps, that the armed forces
were in no condition to run the country and solve its problems. Their
leaders knew nothing about economics, finances, or administration, and
were aware of this. According to politicians, this was enough to stop
them from trying to play any but their traditional strictly professional
role. Besides, there was a kind of sclerosis in the higher ranks of the Army,
and to a certain extent in those of the other branches of the service as
well, which prevented them even from running themselves with the efficiency required of a modern organization. If they couldn't handle their
own interests and assume their responsibilities in a rational way, how
could they dream of taking over the government?

In his usual outspoken way, Edward Korry, the U. S. ambassador in
Chile, expressed to officials of the Foreign Ministry the opinion that the
Chilean government was to blame for the Tacna uprising because it had
not given enough thought to the economic and social situation of the
armed forces or to their structure; but that the Army was to be blamed

even more for not knowing how to manage its financial resources and sensibly use them to purchase armaments and other goods from the United States, for example.

Viaux had found an excuse for his coup in the military's poor economic situation as well as in its errors and deficiencies in establishing a program for the purchase of equipment. Korry's opinion aside, the United States undoubtedly knew more about the problems of the Chilean armed forces than Frei himself; it sized up the situation immediately, and from then on began working out a definite plan to make the most of the dissatisfaction among the military which the Tacna coup had brought to light. There is even reason to believe that the United States knew about this coup before it happened. For one thing, Agustín Edwards had known about it ahead of time and had traveled to Washington. The work of the American military missions in Chile, the bilateral relations between the two countries, and the Pentagon's close watch on Chile from the beginning of the sixties gave the United States more insight into Chile's armed forces than its own civil authorities in Santiago had, and even more than the top brass of the separate branches of these forces, coordinated by a rickety General Staff that was more a front than something viable.

The clearest example of how quickly the United States exploited the weak situation of the Chilean armed forces is revealed by a curious episode which occurred partly in Chile and partly in the United States in early 1970, a few months after the "Tacnazo." The presidential campaign was in full swing, with Salvador Allende, Radimiro Tomic, and Jorge Alessandri fighting it out. Suddenly, there appeared mysterious signs of an attempt by the military, instigated by the United States, to bring off a coup and prevent the elections. Little space was given to this in the news, yet it probably caused Chile more political anxiety and genuine fear than the revolt of the Tacna regiment. Some of the leading Christian Democrats were so worried that they seriously thought of going into exile, and several emissaries went abroad to prepare the way for them. Perhaps President Eduardo Frei considered this possibility, but it would be difficult to find that out now.

The coup did not take place. What happened? Several top Christian Democrats (Senator Renan Fuentealba and other members of the government, including the foreign minister), on the basis of strong and precise indications, publicly condemned the United States as the instigator of the embryonic attempt and denounced the CIA's part in it.[3]

The angry denunciation of the subversive maneuvers of the United

States to precipitate a coup in complicity with the Chilean Army was repeated by high government officials and other political figures in Washington itself. The affair seemed quite serious to certain U. S. Democratic senators, like Eugene McCarthy, who noted that — according to his own knowledge about American action in Chile — the number of CIA and military personnel operating there, apart from those attached to the U. S. embassy, exceeded by far the "normal" number required.

The impact of these charges was serious enough to persuade the government in Washington to cancel the operation. The embryonic coup fell through. However, it clearly showed how decisive and important American participation in a military coup could be. After all, the United States did not yet believe that Allende had a serious chance to win the elections. According to the CIA (in the real meaning of the name, this time) and the opinion polls it was conducting in Chile, the reactionary Alessandri would win the election — the only sure guarantee for the complete protection of U. S. interests in Chile. And at the American Metal Market Copper Forum in New York City on June 12, 1970, Ferrer, one of the leading representatives of U. S. investors in Latin America, assured those present that he had good reasons to believe that if Alessandri were elected there would be no change in Chile's attitude toward the mining industry.

Aside from Ambassador Korry's profuse declarations prior to the elections revealing this prediction as favorable to Alessandri, the existence and results of CIA polls were officially confirmed by Senate hearings conducted in 1973 by Senator Frank Church to investigate ITT's behavior in Chile. In his book *The Sovereign State of ITT*, Anthony Sampson cites the results of the opinion polls as among the first of a series of informational exchanges between the U. S. government and this multinational company. According to Sampson, in early 1970 Harold Geneen, president of ITT, and his colleague on the board of directors, John McCone (ex-director of the CIA, who was still a consultant for the agency while working for ITT), had been concerned about Chile's future, had raised the subject at board meetings, and had discussed it between themselves. They both believed Allende could not be beaten in the elections. McCone discussed this with CIA Director Richard Helms, who had once worked under him and was still his friend. He had checked with Helms several times, in Washington and at McCone's own home in California, to see if the U. S. government had decided to do anything to boost a friendly candidate in Chile. Helms said that the 40 Committee (a part of the National Security Council, headed by

Kissinger) had decided not to do anything at that time. Estimates varied
on the outcome of the elections and the CIA had conducted its own
poll, which predicted that Jorge Alessandri, the favorite, would win the
plurality with 40 percent of the votes.[4]

Helms, however, told McCone that he did not think Alessandri had a
chance to win; in any case, a "minimal effort" to oppose Allende would
be made by the CIA, since the elasticity of its budget left room for this.
In turn, McCone suggested that someone from the CIA should speak to
the president of ITT about this. As a result, Helms asked William Broe,
the CIA's director of clandestine activities in Latin America, to get in
touch with Geneen. The interview took place on July 16, 1970, at the
Sheraton Carlton, an ITT hotel, in Washington. The fact of operations
(both joint and separate) by the CIA and ITT was amply demonstrated
at the Senate hearings by statements from McCone, Broe, Korry, Merriam,
Gerrity, and Geneen, among others. These activities included economic,
financial, political, and terrorist sabotage, carried out in order to provoke
subversion and launch a civil war.

One example of this can be found in the report on Chile of September
17, 1970, addressed to ITT's Vice-President Gerrity, which says in sections 5 and 6:

> . . . some degree of bloodshed seems inevitable. Is the Chilean
> military capable of coping with nationwide violence or a civil
> war? Opinion is divided on this in Santiago. Korry has said he
> considers the armed forces a 'bunch of toy soldiers.' Well-
> informed Chileans and some U. S. advisers believe the army and
> national police have the capability. There are definite reserva-
> tions about the air force and navy. We know that the army has
> been assured full material and financial assistance by the U. S.
> military establishment.[5]

These meetings on Chile were begun in July and continued in August.
New conversations took place between Broe (CIA) and Geneen (ITT),
as well as between McCone (ITT) and Helms (CIA). Decisions were
reached in September, right after Allende's victory. After a meeting of
ITT's Board of Directors, Geneen asked McCone to pass on his offer —
which had been made previously to the CIA, in July, with Broe as go-
between — of a sum that ran to seven figures. (The sum of $1 million
came up at the Senate hearings, but actually those seven numbers could
have been anywhere between $1 million and $10 million.) McCone
agreed and traveled to Washington, where he took his offer to CIA Director Helms and Dr. Henry Kissinger. Sampson, who tells all of this in
Chapter 11 of his book, basing the facts chiefly on testimony given at

the Senate hearings, notes, "Kissinger said he would get in touch if there was a plan; but (said McCone) he never did." With "he never did" in mind, perhaps we should recall Senator Church's observation in the course of the hearings: "It is obvious somebody is lying; and we must take a serious view of perjury under oath."

This digression, which takes us from the abortive coup in early 1970, the year of the Chilean elections, to the public accusations of complicity between top officials in Washington (Kissinger) and the highest executives of a multinational company like ITT is not pointless. It shows that the secret subversive practices of the United States are carried out at different levels, and that disclosures about one of these levels do not preclude continued operation at another; the official but more discreet activities of the U. S. government may use other means and follow different plans, but the objective is the same.

Looked at from one angle, exposures like those made by Jack Anderson when he published the "Secret Memos from ITT" and those at the Senate hearings on the activities abroad of multinational corporations (limited here to ITT in Chile) end by relieving the conscience and the political uneasiness of Americans. It makes them think, wrongly, that everything has been cleared up and that the conspiracy between the government and ITT could not have been too serious, because it failed, after all.

In the United States the man in the street is accustomed to sensational political exposés. Checking certain documents and confessions from the Senate hearings, he may even interpret the reticence of this or that official not as wariness, but as proof of incorruptibility. Thus, according to McCone, Dr. Kissinger and ITT had not been in contact about Chile since mid-September 1970, except for a letter dated October 23 from ITT's Vice-President Merriam and enclosed with a report which proposed that Chile be strangled economically and suggested various specific measures against the Allende government. In a letter dated November 9, Kissinger replied that he had read the report carefully and passed it on to the experts on Latin American affairs on his staff. He concluded: "It is very helpful to have your thoughts and recommendations, and we shall certainly take them into account. I am grateful for your taking the time to give them to me." (Commenting on this answer, ITT's vice-president observed to his superior: "Believe this is more than perfunctory. Things are brewing on the Chile matter and will be back to you later on that subject.")

Despite the fact that the ideas suggested in that ITT report were later put into practice by the U. S. government, public opinion outside of Chile seemed to express a certain satisfaction when it finally discovered how the government of a powerful country, working hand in hand with a large multinational company, behaves toward a small country. After all, ITT's most deadly plans, those which would have caused a lot of blood to flow, seemed to have come to nothing.

Still, this impression of knowing what was behind American policy is false. The only things known are what the manipulators of the U. S. political system want known; and that means only specific things that will work in the interests of American policy. The disclosures of the ITT plot against Chile are excellent proof of this, as we shall see.

In fact, these disclosures are far from being the truth about the United States' overall policy toward Chile. The CIA's role in 1970 was relatively secondary; in some cases the most it did was help the United States in its operations, and perhaps it was kept ignorant up to a certain point of the real direction U. S. global policy was taking. Those who defined policy, with Kissinger in the lead, had all the information and made all the key decisions. They were careful, however, not to make any public statements about these decisions, and it was only by accident that incriminating documents signed by them were released. Besides, public officials always come up with a good explanation for what they do. As long as they serve the system faithfully, their supreme power justifies their acts. Their loyalty absolves them.

The plan for intervention in Chile in 1970 was the work of the Pentagon, whose job it also was to carry it out, starting it before the elections and, if necessary, keeping it going through the elections and afterwards. The plot and its plans for operation were a much bigger secret than the activities of ITT and the CIA in Chile had been. The policy decision in this matter had to come from the president. Dr. Kissinger had to have known of the plan and approved of it. But some bureaucrat committed an error that let the Chileans in on part of it.

After the experience of the years 1969-1970 summed up in the preceding pages, which was the latest known phase of U. S. policy in Chile and the rest of Latin America, the Chilean embassy in Washington, from mid-1970 on, decided to keep an eye peeled for anything that looked suspicious, no matter now insignificant. This was intellectually, technically, and politically impossible — like trying to clean out the stables of Augeas in the labyrinth of Knossos. Many things told in this book,

more than three years later, were barely or not at all known then; sometimes they appeared to be mere intuitions or, even worse, inductive or
inconclusive reasoning — and the situation called for scepticism and
prudence.

Some practical steps, however, could be taken. For instance, consular
records could be checked to see how many and what kind of visas to
enter Chile were requested by Americans just before the election. This
work could appear to lead nowhere, since American tourists, according
to a one-way agreement, could go into Chile for brief periods without
any visas. This being the case, what American secret agent would be
stupid enough to leave tracks by going in with a visa?

Yet an incredible thing happened. Some Washington bureaucrat who
did not know the reason for the visit of several groups of U. S. naval
officers to Chile (almost one hundred of them within the space of a few
months toward the middle of 1970) decided to follow regulations and
request visas — obligatory for members of the armed forces from any
country — at the Chilean embassy for them, individually, or in small
groups.

This happened over a period of several weeks. With the help of information from sources which are difficult to retrace, the embassy gathered
enough evidence to justify its political and moral indignation, protested
energetically to the U. S. government, and took the measures the situation required. Foreign Minister Gabriel Valdés had already been tipped
off through regular as well as special channels because of the gravity of
the case. He ordered his office to start an investigation immediately to
find out who, among the navy personnel requesting visas, were already
in Chile, and to check up on all the Americans who had entered the
country during the previous few months. Several things were made clear
by the inquiry, including the fact that none of the naval officers had
entered Chile, although several visas dated back more than a month.
He then told the embassy not to give out any more visas to Americans
and to prevent any more of them from entering Chile. He also gave an
order to protest and demand an explanation from the State Department.

Why give so much importance to these requests for visas that seemed
above suspicion? By going over certain notes made by the Defense Department on the forms asking for the visas, and especially by checking
back through extraofficial channels, the embassy had learned that the
staggered requests for entry visas had been made by a group of officers
and noncoms, mostly in the Navy, who were experts in communications,

logistics, electronics, intelligence, and similar activities. There were naval engineers and pilots among them. Many of their backgrounds included subversive activities in countries where there had been coups precisely at the time of their visits there. They were a highly qualified group, whose technical specialties had nothing ostensibly to do with their visit to Chile or even with the activities of the U. S. permanent naval mission in Chile. Among them there were several commanders and captains, many lieutenants and other officers, and a much larger number of specialized noncommissioned officers. Finally, the U. S. Defense Department had absolutely no publicly known project under-way, either in Chile, in the Antarctic, the South Pole, the South Pacific or the South Atlantic, that could explain or motivate the presence of so many military experts in Chile. At the same time, all the visas were for visits to Chile either on September 4, the day of the presidential elections, or just before or after that date.

After the abortive coup of early 1970, in which American complicity with the would-be Chilean rebels had been cut short by the accusations of several U. S. politicians, the Chilean embassy not only protested and demanded an explanation, but also brought two new charges against the United States. First, certain information was brought to the attention of former Ambassador Ralph Dungan, who meanwhile had become superintendent of education in New Jersey and who, in 1965, had been shocked by Project Camelot. He considered the matter so grave and dangerous that he decided to call the Chilean ambassador, not from his telephone at home nor from his office, but from a public booth; he also prepared to leave for Washington immediately to see Henry Kissinger and some of his friends in the State Department.

The second step was to pass other information to Tad Szulc of the *New York Times*. Szulc, in view of the paper's attitude at the time, realized that the tip-off could be put to effective use as a threat to the administration. He got hold of one of the requests for several visas and contributed some sidelights on several of the naval officers.

It is worthwhile reprinting the whole article that appeared in the *New York Times*. Although it failed to make a splash or get a prominent spot in the paper — or perhaps precisely for those two reasons — it was a good warning signal to the military authorities who were preparing their intervention in Chile. Their conspiracy was not a secret, and public opinion, with the right support from the establishment, could stop it.

U.S. Navy's Visa Requests Worry Chile
by Tad Szulc

Washington, September 4 — The United States Navy has applied for Chilean visas for 87 officers, noncommissioned officers and civilian employes over the last eight months, a development that has left the Chilean Government deeply worried.

The situation has been compounded by an apparent breakdown in communications between the State and Defense Departments and by contradictory information subsequently given to the Chileans.

The Government there has been highly sensitive over the presidential election today, and the slightest hint of possible outside interference has aroused great concern.

As a result Chile has directed high-level inquiries to the United States Government about the planned visits by naval personnel.

At one point the Chileans were told that the visa applicants made up a Navy band — an explanation that they did not believe and that was later withdrawn.

Last week the Chilean Embassy held up the granting of the last batch of 19 visa requests. Sixty-eight had already been granted. Most of those involved are now believed to be on assignment elsewhere.

The Chilean election had been considered the most important in Latin America in recent years because one of the candidates, Dr. Salvador Allende, was a Marxist whose victory would bring to power the first democratically elected Marxist regime in the Western Hemisphere.

While the first visa for a civilian employe was requested by the Bureau of Naval Personnel last Jan. 5 and further requests were made subsequently, the Chilean Government became suspicious of what it believed to be a pattern. The three latest lists were submitted last week.

The lists of applicants, sent to the Chilean Embassy by the Navy Department, were not made available to the State Department at the time because the military services usually bypass the department on matters they consider routine.

Only after Chile complained did the State Department ask the Navy for an explanation and identification of those for whom visas had been requested. The lists were made available to The New York Times by official sources.

Under existing practice the military usually state no reason for the travel for which visas are requested. Letters accompanying the applications to Chile requested visas for "travel on official duty for the Navy Department in Chile."

Last Thursday the Chilean Foreign Ministry asked for an explanation from the United States Ambassador, Edward M. Korry.

According to diplomatic informants, Mr. Korry and the office of the United States naval attaché in Santiago were unfamiliar with the applications and could not provide answers.

Inquiries by the embassy here last weekend elicited from the State Department the explanation that the visas were for a Navy band to be sent on a goodwill tour.

Chilean Embassy officials expressed surprise because there was no record that such a visit was planned. They also noted that the ranks of the men involved made it unlikely that they were musicians.

The 87 applicants consisted of 3 captains, 3 commanders, 15 lieutenant commanders, 8 lieutenants, 2 lieutenants junior grade, 1 ensign, 1 midshipman, 2 chief warrant officers, 45 chief petty officers and petty officers, 1 boiler tender and 6 civilian employes.

On Monday the State Department told the embassy that the information concerning the band was erroneous. The department said that the Navy had reported that of the 87 applications 38 were for personnel assigned to United States bases in the Antarctic and 49 in support of Operation Unitas, an annual exercise in anti-submarine warfare.

The operation has been conducted for years in conjunction with a number of Latin-American navies, including Chile's. Several months ago, however, Chile's participation was cancelled to avoid the possibility that the presence of American warships in Chilean waters would be interpreted as a sign of United States political pressure.

In response to inquiries today, a Navy Department spokesman said that Chile granted 85 visas in 1968 and 64 last year. Commenting on this year's applications, the spokesman said that "visas have been requested for crews of two patrol aircraft and one logistics back-up aircraft for use in the event of emergencies in the Unitas operation." He added: "Unless there is an emergency the visas will not be used."

Both the Navy spokesman and a spokesman for the State Department, who said that the visa requests had been routine, were unable to clarify why Unitas personnel were needed in Chile this year in view of the cancellation.

The Navy spokesman said that visas for personnel engaged in Antarctic operations were needed during the "summer support season." The Antarctic summer begins in December. Palmer Base, a United States installation in the Antarctic, is supplied through Punta Arenas, a Chilean port on the strait of Magellan.

The normal complement at Palmer, the Navy said, is 10 men. The Chileans raised the question why 38 were needed for rotation and resupply.

Records at the Defense Department disclosed that several of the officers for whom visas were asked hold academic degrees in physical, space, aeroengineering and computer sciences and marine biology. The list included a naval architect.

All the officers are classified as "unrestricted line officers," meaning that they can be called upon for any duty. A number are naval aviators, several are qualified as destroyer and submarine commanders and at least one took graduate studies in defense intelligence.

It is a Government practice to request visas for military personnel, who carry official passports.

The requests to Chile were in some instances for three months and in others for a year, involving "repeated trips." [*New York Times*, Sept. 5, 1970][6]

Meanwhile, a little drama was being acted out in Washington by the Chilean embassy and the U. S. State Department. The embassy announced that it was seriously concerned and wondered why such a large group of officers and other specialists in the U. S. Navy wanted to visit Chile at that precise time for a visit to the U. S. naval mission, an inspection trip, training or tourism, a short stopover, etc. The State Department seemed surprised, even incredulous, answering that it knew nothing about the matter but would check with the Defense Department. The inquiries there dragged on, and the embassy complained again. The State Department replied that it had not been able to learn anything from Defense. The embassy insisted that it could not accept this explanation since the Pentagon had indeed asked for a large number of visas, and the embassy could not understand why all those officers wanted to go to Chile; somebody should clear things up. Then the embassy decided to go straight to the Pentagon. The State Department suddenly telephoned to say that they had figured it out, and that two officials would be sent over with the explanation. This was at the very moment that Valdés decided, in Chile, not to let any more Americans into the country. The two officials arrived at the Chilean embassy that same afternoon, carrying several folders filled with papers. They looked nervous, and as if they had just lost their best friend. They were underlings from the "Chile" section of the department. Ambassador Santa María turned the interview over to his counselor, Armando Uribe.

The American officials explained that everything was clear. The U. S. naval officers and noncoms were going to Chile to take part in the joint naval maneuvers, Operation Unitas. The counselor answered that the U. S. government had known for months that those maneuvers had been

cancelled that year because of the presidential elections on September 4.
The officials glanced at each other and, after an embarrassing moment,
the older of the two spoke up to say that the counselor had not quite
understood what they meant. The navy men were the members of the
Navy Band of the units taking part in Operation Unitas; although Chile
would not participate in the maneuvers because of the elections, the
band intended to visit Chile as a gesture of friendship during the Peru-
United States naval exercises in September. The counselor had a quick
reply. First, he knew that this gesture of friendship had not been scheduled by the two governments, and that this was the first news received
of any musical intentions. Second, he had never heard of any Navy
band with so many commanders, officers, lieutenants, noncoms, and
specialists of every rank. And finally, he was very familiar with the
Operation Unitas Navy Band and knew that it was not made up of those
navy people who had asked for visas to go to Chile. There was a silence
that lasted several seconds. One of the two finally found his tongue and
said that they would pass this information on to their superiors. They
left.

John Crimmins, assistant secretary of state for Latin America, received the Chilean ambassador and his counselor shortly after this.

Crimmins said that there had been a regrettable misunderstanding —
a terrible bureaucratic mixup; no Unitas Navy Band ever intended to
visit Chile. He explained that the officers, noncoms, and others for
whom the Defense Department had solicited visas were all going to
Chile for different reasons: some, just a few, intended to visit the
naval mission in Chile; a larger number were just passing through, on
their way to American bases in the Antarctic; a few others wanted
a visa to stop over on their way to other countries, like Argentina and
Brazil. But most of them, he added, were attached to ships that would
soon take part in the Peruvian-American naval maneuvers and, in such
cases, the Defense Department would get them visas for all the neighboring countries, in case they wanted to visit them.

Crimmins's broad face was dead serious as he reeled off his speech in
a monotone. In conclusion, he informed the ambassador that the department had let the Pentagon know that it would like the Navy men's visits
to Chile canceled.

There was no need to know anything else. This was more than
enough. The Navy Band incident was over, and the operation canceled.

That's what we thought in August 1970. Although a Chilean admiral,
whose conduct in this affair seemed questionable, was retired a short
time later, Captain Arturo Troncoso remained at his post in the embassy.

We have already mentioned that Troncoso would lead the uprising of
1973 in Valparaiso, where the coup was to be launched on September 11.
He had already met in 1969 with American officers in Washington to
talk about Chile's internal affairs; another participant had been the owner
of *El Mercurio*, Agustín Edwards. Shortly after the coup, in an interview for *Le Monde*, Troncoso boasted about his excellent relations with
the United States and his admiration for that country. General Ernesto
Baeza also remained at his post in Washington. As a military attaché
there in 1970, he was, even then, an unconditional enemy of Communism; for him, a worldwide armed struggle between the positive forces of
"democracy" and the negative forces of "Communism" was inevitable;
it was already underway in each and every corner of the globe and
would continue until one side won. The front line of this mortal struggle
passed right through Chile, and the general used to trace it on the map
of South America with a pointer. One felt like smiling at his simplistic
demonstration then. But he was shrewd and seemed to change his geo-
political attitude in the next few months. It was true that he had good
friends in the Pentagon (he had said so in a conversation on June 24,
1970), but that did not mean that he saw eye-to-eye with all of them
on everything. . . . On September 11, 1973, General Baeza led the
armed attack on La Moneda Palace where President Allende held out
until his death. Today he is the junta's director of national security.

5

U. S. policy toward Chile and specifically the measures against the Allende administration which were formulated at the highest government level — the National Security Council and the 40 Committee headed by Kissinger and with Nixon occasionally in attendance — were redefined five times between 1970 and 1973, according to documents now available. Since these are secret decisions and theoretically are not made known — except, in the long run, by their end results — the dates applied to each are approximate — although, with the exception of the first, they are probably exact. The first four measures were adopted in 1970, which shows that the Americans were not sure how to go about preventing Allende's election and, later on, toppling the legitimate Chilean government. The first was adopted some time before the middle of 1970; the second, on September 14 or 15; the third, between November 1 and 5; and the fourth, either on the 5th or 6th. The final measure before the coup of September 11, 1973, was decided on between March 4 and 24 of that year.

Evidence of these high-level policy decisions (the common denominator in U. S. global strategy as applied to Chile has been the invariable and decisive presence of Dr. Kissinger) comes from several sources. For the first decision, we have McCone's testimony on March 21, 1973, at the Senate hearings presided over by Senator Frank Church. (There are no other sources, and the real nature of the measures taken in mid-1970 has not been proved beyond a doubt; odd, considering the general suspicions McCone's declarations aroused in the Senators. For instance,

51

quoting his personal friend Helms, the head of the CIA, McCone described U. S. policy as benevolent, and spoke of Helms — and, inciden-
tally, of Kissinger and Nixon, his friend and fellow Republican — in a
more or less favorable light, although this assessment did not fit in with
what happened then and later.)

For the sources on the decisions taken by the 40 Committee around
September 14, there are several declarations made before the Senate subcommittee[1] that are substantiated by Dr. Kissinger's "briefing" on September 16 in Chicago and illustrated by the revelations contained in the
ITT memo of September 17 (a photocopy of which was published by
the Chilean government). According to this memo, "Late Tuesday
night (September 15) Ambassador Edward Korry finally received a message from State Department giving him the green light to move in the
name of President Nixon. The message gave him maximum authority to
do all possible — short of a Dominican Republic-type action — to keep
Allende from taking power."

The third decision, in early November 1970, can be considered together with the fourth one which followed right after it on November 5
or 6. We can differentiate them because Charles Meyer, assistant secretary of state for Latin America, was present when the latter was made
and had a hand in it. He had just returned to Washington from Santiago,
where he had attended Allende's inauguration. This fourth decision
defined a more flexible policy than the hard line adopted at the very
beginning of the month, which had called for more direct subversive
methods, along the tough lines suggested by the CIA on September 29
through its representative, William Broe.[2] But other indications give
an even better picture of the measures adopted by the United States
in early November and of the two adopted by the Security Council
after that: they are, the events during Assistant Secretary of State
Meyer's visit to Chile, his sudden return to Washington (under circumstances that will be examined later), and the subsequent discoveries
made by Chile's foreign minister.

Finally, our information on the last decision made by Kissinger and
the American government in mid-March 1973, adopting a hard-line
policy toward Chile, comes directly from leading decision-makers in
the State Department, who got together toward the end of the month
with the Chilean delegation for the second round of conversations
about pending legal hassles. This delegation was headed by Ambassador
Orlando Letelier (who was arrested by the junta after the coup), and
another of its members was Deputy Luis Maira. They faced the assistant
secretary of state for Latin America, John Crimmins.

Now that we have mentioned these dates and sources, let us study each decision.

In his declaration before the Senate subcommittee, which we have already seen in part, McCone stated that CIA Director Richard Helms told him in mid-1970 that the 40 Committee, under Kissinger, had decided some time before not to do anything about the elections in Chile, but that "a 'minimal effort' to oppose Allende *would* be managed within the flexibility of the CIA budget."[3] This would-be decision was picked up on June 29, 1970, by J. M. Navasal, a newsman for *El Mercurio*, from the mouth of a State Department official — probably Charles Meyer — who had told the journalist: "The result of the presidential election will undoubtedly express the will of the Chilean people. We would be pleased, as I have already said, if it should coincide with our point of view. But if it should differ, if a candidate opposed to the democratic principles we sustain were elected, we would have to accept that verdict as the free decision of the Chilean people. We would regret it, but we would respect such a decision." This was the official facade of U.S. policy toward Chile before the elections. But behind this facade, as revealed in the words of the expert on Chilean matters, Joseph Jova, on December 31, 1969, it is possible to detect a less conciliatory line. Further behind the facade, Director Helms had told ex-Director of the CIA McCone — a "multinational" man — that his agency would make at least a minimal effort, within the flexibility of its budget, to oppose Allende. And even further behind, the Pentagon, outlining its own careful plan of intervention, had attempted to send to Chile almost one hundred specialists in subversion. . . .

What was the United States' real policy toward Chile? In a way, it fit all three of the phases just mentioned. Each was a pretext or cover-up for the one following, and the last justified and completed the one preceding. A complex system, it is based on a compartmentalized bureaucracy. But at the top of the pyramid of power, the false illusions and deceptive fronts, dominating all the labyrinths, was Dr. Kissinger, President Nixon's operator and master strategist of U. S. foreign policy — and he is still there.

The following confidential memorandum of August 1970, drawn up in Washington by Chilean sources for general background, will help us understand better what was really going on:

> On the surface, the U. S. government is calm about the 1970 election in Chile. From what we know of that government's traditional operating methods, it is certain that, under this calm

surface, secret analyses are being made of plans for action and reaction, and preparations may even be under way to put some of these into effect.

The agencies in charge of this work are probably the Defense Department (the Defense Intelligence Agency), the State Department, the CIA, and the White House. The National Security Council is no doubt the coordinator and decision-making organization; the final decisions are, of course, President Nixon's. We can safely guess that in each of these agencies there are special staffs and task forces in charge of working out the analyses and suitable plans.

With regard to Chile, the position of the U. S. government does not seem to be very coherent. It is possible that the State Department acts or believes it is acting in accordance with one policy and that this appears to be the government's official position, while other U. S. agencies have very different policies of their own. The State Department's official stand, which it partially acknowledges, is to keep its hands off, no matter what happens in Chile. Yet it seems very unlikely, or rather impossible, that the State Department — and, of course, other U. S. government agencies as well — has not worked out some plan of action to tackle events in Chile. Considering the way the United States has operated in the past, these plans probably are open to change, with leeway for alternative action depending on the turn of events.

From what we know of the Nixon administration — its policy makers, its structure, its international actions, its "doctrines" — and of the domestic political situation of the United States, this government, even before it makes any decisions, is likely to make declarations or take definite action against Chile, then wait to see what actually happens. This does not mean that it relies on improvisation; on the contrary, every possible hypothesis is taken into account, but its decisions are made to look like *reactions* to whatever occurs.

It is therefore unlikely that the United States will take any steps *before* the Chilean elections. It is more probable that it will act *during* election time (from the time of the ballot count until the ratification of the election by Congress), though it is doubtful that the United States will make any move unless something grave happens (like a coup d'etat). It is even more likely that the Americans will act when the new government in Chile is formed. (For instance, there may be statements, which are more or less official, if the Communist party becomes part of the government, but there would probably only be declarations of this type, at this stage.) On the other hand, in response to certain actions of the

new Chilean government, the United States may make formal
statements or take steps through secret, or even through official,
economic measures, or through private or public diplomatic
agreements with other countries, etc.

The purpose of this study is to trace, on the basis of what we
know has happened in the past, a series of measures the Chilean
government might decide to take and the corresponding reactions
of the United States.

1. American investors apparently support Alessandri with
money, but the U. S. government stays out of it.

2. That government will probably follow a "wait-and-see"
policy until after the elections, the new government's take-over,
and its subsequent actions, since any American interference would
have to be justified before the Chilean people as well as other
nations, and this can only be done if the United States seems to
be reacting to specific acts that affect its interests or threaten it.

3. If Alessandri is elected, the United States will give him
strong financial, economic, and political support, and will provide
him with advice and the means to control the internal trouble
that he will surely face (terrorism in the cities, social unrest, political resistance, etc.). This support would justify and facilitate any
strong-arm tactics by Alessandri's regime and, in case of need,
could even incite them.

4. If Alessandri cannot control the situation, the United States
probably has plans ready to back a military coup. Such a coup
would have one of three objectives: (a) to call for new elections,
controlled by the military, with all the leftist parties banned from
participating; (b) to implement immediate takeover by a rightist
military government, backed by procapitalist factions; (c) to
implement immediate takeover by a dictatorship, military or otherwise, of the pseudo-Left, which would take certain measures that
would appear anti-American, but which, at the same time, would
give solid political and economic guarantees to the United States.

5. If Tomic were elected, the United States would try, while
the government was being formed, to reach a tacit or expressed
agreement to keep Popular Unity from direct or indirect participation, and to put a limit on the government's power to take
measures, both domestic (such as nationalizations) and foreign (in
relation to Cuba, the OAS, etc.). If an agreement were not reached,
the United States would wait for the government to take some
step that would justify reactions on its part. These reactions will
be explained later.

6. If Allende is elected, the United States probably has plans
for immediate action to annul the election results. These plans

would fit in with one of the three alternatives in hypothesis number 4, above. But it would probably "wait and see" for the reasons expressed in hypothesis 2.

7. If the Allende government can count on the direct or indirect participation of Tomic's forces, the reaction of the United States may be slower in coming, but in any case it probably will be the same kind of reaction. Of course, before any of the possibilities in hypothesis 4 take place, there will probably be a short period during which the Chilean government will be treated as "illegitimate." This will be interpreted through official statements issued by the United States; diplomatic or political consultations (bilateral or in the OAS) with Latin American countries; ecomonic sanctions; instigation of internal dissension; accusations against Chile of meddling in the affairs of other countries; etc.

8. What measures by the Chilean government would lead to American interference?

a. Total nationalization of American interests in Chile without equitable, rapid, and effective indemnification. Keep in mind that this concept of indemnification is relative. There have been almost no examples of nationalization during the last twenty-five years in which indemnification has fulfilled these three demands. It is also noteworthy that once certain limits — which are not defined a priori — are crossed, it is practically the same thing as not paying any indemnification; for example, an indemnification of less than 40 percent of what the United States considers an equitable price will probably be considered a complete refusal to indemnify.

b. Declarations or actions that the United States interprets as supporting "subversion" in other Latin American countries.

c. Any kind of military pact with the USSR, China, Cuba, or perhaps other socialist countries.

9. It would be difficult to predict U. S. reaction to some of these measures, for example: collectivization of means of production (this would probably follow the nationalization already mentioned); important agreements to export copper to China; imposing a political ideology on the armed forces; etc.

10. In reference to the measures of the Chilean government enumerated in item 8 — especially nationalization, the one most likely to occur — we have to make a distinction about the possible reactions of the United States. If this measure is sufficiently "isolated," if it is not accompanied simultaneously by the others listed in item 9, American interference may be relatively limited. This means that as long as it is clear that this measure would not be immediately followed by others that would affect interests considered vital by the United States (for example, U. S. security interests affected by Chilean support of subversion in other coun-

tries or by direct military pacts with socialist countries), U. S. reaction would probably only be to (a) "denounce" this measure internationally as a violation of international rights; (b) apply its domestic laws to establish economic sanctions against Chile; or (c) make financial reprisals through public and private banking agencies. The second reaction would probably not come into play if the nationalization were seen in such a light as to cast a kind of "shadow" on the indemnification that made economic sanctions of the United States seem excessive or unjust. On the other hand, these sanctions against Chile could be swung in its favor, since they could very well justify a decision on Chile's part to take "reprisals," and support its right, internationally, to take some of the other measures (mentioned in items 8 and 9) that would consolidate the government's position at home and abroad.

11. It follows from this, that Chile must be prepared to take certain actions. (a) During the elections, and especially once the new government has been formed and is taking the first steps that, in the eyes of the United States, can harm its interests, we must watch out that Washington does not set up any of the situations listed in item 4. This should lead to the immediate formation of an intelligence system to offset this danger and stir up public opinion against it. Yet it is doubtful whether it would be a good thing to create a climate of apprehension that might turn into an internal political issue and precipitate action by the United States. (b) It may be advisable to keep up appearances by separating nationalizations from other measures, leaving them for later, so that the government could stand up internationally to the United States, and even use it to justify other measures Chile might want to take. (c) Nationalizations should be prepared so that they may be seen in a favorable light by other countries. This does not mean that the indemnifications considered "equitable" by the United States must be acknowledged as such or even paid; it means that we must count on as many legal, economic, and political arguments as possible in order to receive international support for each nationalization. In other words, to present it as a nationalization and not as a "confiscation," for in the latter case, we would lose important means of legal defense and international action that would allow us to gain precious time. That is why we mentioned above the usefulness of presenting nationalization in such a way as to cast a "shadow" around the question of indemnification. (d) Chile must be prepared to react against U. S. economic sanctions. (e) It must be ready to confront the financial reprisals the United States can launch through international banking organizations like the World Bank, IDB, Eximbank, and private American and European banks.

The original of this memorandum (the final version reached President Allende during the elections) has probably suffered the fate of the presidential files, destroyed when Allende's home and office were attacked and demolished by the counterrevolutionaries.

The elections on September 4, 1970, gave Salvador Allende the relative plurality. The events of the next days in Chile are well known, and the actions of the Chilean right wing and the American embassy in Santiago are very vividly described in the ITT reports published in the "Secret Memos." Those documents and the Senate hearings in 1973 also shed light on some of the secret activities organized in the United States after the Chilean elections. But in Washington a number of other events, never written down, also took place.

For example, Peter Vaky, former assistant secretary of state for Latin America, who was then a member of Kissinger's team in the National Security Council, was in a hurry to complete the studies on Allende that Kissinger had requested. Vaky not only made comments that appear in the ITT report for September 14 addressed to Vice-President Merriam (for instance, "Mr. Vaky said there has been 'lots of thinking' about the Chile situation and that it is a 'real tough one' for the U. S."), but he also told other persons that he was putting together, in the White House, a thorough study of Allende and the Popular Unity party. All of Allende's speeches, statements, and known activities were being processed by computers.

But Vaky may have become a victim, around that time, of one of Kissinger's sudden fits of temper, because a rumor started circulating in Washington that Vaky was about to leave the White House (which he did) and that he would be replaced by Korry; instead, his place was taken by Arnold Nachmanoff, an official in the National Security Council. In any event, perhaps driven by the pressures of his work or by Kissinger's demands, Vaky was unable to hide his personal hostility toward Allende and Popular Unity, and a kind of horror of the Chilean Communist party — feelings that anticipated, in a primitive way, the position his superior would soon take.

At this time, as the ITT Report for October 21 revealed much later, the struggle between the U. S. ambassador to Chile, Edward Korry, and the State Department caused Korry to call the White House frequently to provide it with apocalyptic reports and analyses on what was to come. (Korry's role and personality will be examined separately.) One commentary from John Fisher, director of the State Department's Bureau of

Andean and Pacific Affairs, stated on September 16 that "Ambassador Korry is fully convinced that if Allende becomes President there will be no half measures — the country will be communist controlled."[4]

A few months before the elections, Korry had committed himself by personally informing Washington that Alessandri would be the winner and that he was sure Allende would not be elected. When Allende was elected on September 4, Korry, overstepping his official duties, made it a point to put pressure on Chile to reverse the election results and stop Allende from becoming president.[5] It may seem paradoxical to anyone who is unfamiliar with the preeminently bureaucratic structure of power in Washington, but Korry applied some of this pressure on his own superiors in the government, in order to make them adopt a policy in line with his own views and their implementation; he did this so that he would be covered and backed up in his actions and his official duties. In other words, he turned in reports that justified what he had already done and what he was continuing to do. Involved for many months in the struggle for power between the White House and the State Department — a struggle that had its crucial moments in 1970, before Kissinger's victory had been decided — Korry had made an obvious exhibition of going over to Kissinger's team. Consequently, his reports were aimed at reinforcing what he considered to be the White House's hard line and, on the other hand, criticizing the State Department's instructions before and during the Chilean elections. In effect, his opinions "nourished" (something Kissinger and Nixon appreciated) certain aggressive tendencies in American policy toward Chile in the months following September 4.[6]

Clear proof that this was the attitude adopted by the White House, was revealed by the passages dedicated to Chile by Dr. Kissinger in his famous "background briefing" in September 1970 before representatives of the Chicago press. Kissinger's words, quoted again and again in newspaper commentaries during the past three years (and almost never mentioning his name in accordance with this curious American institution of the "background"), were made in response to questions asked about the significance that the election of Allende had on the United States.

The literal transcription of the questions and answers circulated throughout Latin America and Europe; of course, one could only then reveal Kissinger's words with caution, without citing the complete text and without attributing it to him. Several journalists (including certain foreign correspondents) obtained transcripts. One copy reached *Le Monde* in Paris. The Chilean ambassador to Washington was able to procure another copy, but, due to the coup of September 11, its fate is unknown.

A partial quote from the transcript, printed by the U. S. government, enables us to reconstitute some of the main points:

> So I don't think we should delude ourselves that an Allende take-over in Chile would not present massive problems for us, and for democratic forces and for pro-U. S. forces in Latin America, and indeed to the whole Western Hemisphere. What would happen to the Western Hemisphere Defense Board, or to the Organization of American States, and so forth, is extremely problematical. So we are taking a close look at the situation. It is not one in which our capacity for influence is very great at this particular moment now that matters have reached this particular point.[7]

What is missing from this transcript, however, is one very fundamental point made by Kissinger at that briefing: namely, that the political evolution of Chile would be very serious for the interests of U. S. national security because of its effects on France and Italy.[8]

Kissinger's warnings were made on September 16, 1970. His ideas were picked up in 1971 and 1972 by political columnists not only in South America but also in New York, Washington, Europe, and even in Hong Kong in October 1973. One of the first to use them was the shrewd veteran reporter Cyrus Sulzberger of the *New York Times*. He caught the essential strategy behind Kissinger's statements: the repercussions of the Chilean events on Italy and France. That is why he published on January 13, 1971, his famous article "Spaghetti with Chile Sauce," which was still stirring up newspaper commentaries and rebuttals three years later.[9]

Sulzberger was one of the first newpapermen to become alarmed by Popular Unity, and he sounded the alarm. With his elder statesman-journalist style — in the tradition of Walter Lippmann, but much more conservative and less brilliant — and making the most of his connections within political and governmental circles, Sulzberger had made a big fuss, a few days after the Chilean election, about the danger of Chile becoming, like Cuba, a potential base for Soviet submarines. Soon after, a spokesman for the Pentagon made an identical statement in Washington, obviously intended to affect the Chilean electoral process, whose definite result, following the ballot-count on September 4, then depended on the constitutional ratification by Congress of Allende's election.[10] There is no doubt that Sulzberger, like Joseph Kraft (who publicly said so during his visit to Chile shortly after Allende's rise to power) and other handpicked newsmen, had conversations with Kissinger about Chile during the key period in which U. S. policy toward Chile was being worked out; a two-way current of influence flowed between these men, who represented a significant fraction of the American establishment, and the White House. Kissinger influenced them and they influenced him.

The only thing of lasting value in Kissinger's world view — which included Chile in the scheme of international strategy — is precisely that treated by Sulzberger: the projection of Chile's experience to West European countries. It seems strange that, during the last three years, other American and European newsmen who knew about the transcript of the Chicago conference have not probed deeply into this question. Perhaps it is a taboo subject, so delicate and fundamental that Kissinger does not like to have it discussed openly. On the other hand, it is referred to in one of the few passages in his secret Chicago briefing that concerned a proven fact.

For it appears that Dr. Kissinger does not always tell the truth, not even in secret to those he trusts. Thus, his remarks on this same occasion ("So we are taking a close look at the situation. It is not one in which our capacity for influence is very great at this particular moment") seem equivocal, at least in the light of the ITT memos, which are more trustworthy because their disclosure was less guarded. We know that somewhere between the day of the elections (September 4) and the day before the briefings (the 15th), the top U. S. policy makers on international questions had gotten together under Kissinger's direction and had made very important decisions concerning Chile. Among the immediate consequences of these decisions of the 40 Committee were instructions sent to Ambassador Korry in Santiago, which he received on the night of the 15th — leading us to believe that these decisions were made some time before then, and that Kissinger's own remarks about Chile, in Chicago, gave only some idea of the reasons behind his policy toward Chile. There is no doubt that it was a strong policy of all-out intervention in Chile, short of bringing in thousands of troops, as Lyndon Johnson had done in 1965 in the Dominican Republic. But this still left a very wide margin for intervention, including every imaginable kind of sabotage and terrorism to provoke political, economic, and internal military subversion, without excluding the mobilization of other countries against Chile.[11]

It is clear then that Dr. Kissinger was not quite truthful when he put on his show of academic scepticism about the United States' "capacity for influence," since he had already made up his mind to carry out major acts of aggression. These included a complete plan for systematically creating an economic crisis in Chile;[12] at the same time, specific instructions were sent to Ambassador Korry giving him "the green light" to act in Nixon's name, with the maximum authority to do everything — "short of a Dominican Republic-type action"—to stop Allende from assuming power.[13]

In short, by mid-September 1970 the U. S. government had officially adopted a policy of all-out intervention in Chile. This policy had been formulated by Dr. Kissinger in President Nixon's name. Official American policy anticipated subversive action of every kind (excluding the massive introduction of troops from the United States) and a systematic plan to provoke economic chaos in Chile, with the aid of private corporations like ITT. (The plan sent to ITT on September 29 by Broe was accompanied by a list of American firms that might cooperate.) In other words, the "ITT plot in Chile," which definitely existed, was only one part of the larger plot hatched by the United States government in Chile.

6

What happened in Chile from mid-September to the end of October 1970, when the accession to power of Allende and Popular Unity hung in the balance, has been described many times. The maneuvers of the right wing ranged from formulas for political sleight of hand (like the proposal that Congress elect Alessandri provided he promise to resign immediately, thereby paving the way for new general elections in which Frei would be a shoo-in) to acts of terrorism by the far Right, which would provoke the reaction of the far Left. This would bring on the expected military intervention, which, in turn, would make new elections possible; here again, Frei would be the victor. Officers of the armed forces were also approached in an attempt to persuade them to organize a coup without seeking any pretext whatever. Other considerations were: plots led by certain Army elements, like the infamous Roberto Viaux and others more obscure and therefore more dangerous; financial and economic operations that would upset the monetary system, production, and distribution; the building up of a climate of distrust and insecurity, with violent methods and psychological tools; terrorist attempts and threats against leftist leaders; and, as a last resort, the assassination of the commander-in-chief of the Army.

All this is familiar. But what has not been clearly seen, in spite of the light thrown on it by the ITT memos, is the close relation between these acts and the policy worked out before September 15, at the top levels of the U. S. government, against Chile. The right wing, the eternal allies of the United States in Chile, did know in good time about this

official American policy and acted accordingly. At the same time, the
ITT documents record in an irrefutable manner American aggression and
the maneuvers of the Chilean reactionaries, and how they plotted hand
in hand.[1] American aggression is not carried out in a vacuum; it needs
accomplices on the inside.

But this aggression is worked out in secret. Neither the men behind
it nor their accomplices go around discussing it, and it is almost impossible to bring it out into the open. Sampson's analysis shows amply how
difficult it is to do this, even when one has plenty of evidence to work
from, as in Chile's case after the publication of the ITT memos and the
Senate hearings in 1973 (although the United States produced these
documents for equivocal reasons, as we shall see). Although he had
enough data to reveal the existence of a U. S. policy that spawned or
encouraged events in Chile, this experienced author, ignoring the evidence, stated, "Exactly who was making United States foreign policy
toward Chile at this time is the crucial unanswered question." He was
referring to events right around September 16. The representatives from
the government and the private corporations, who revealed their inter-
ventionist activities before Church's subcommittee, had been very
skillful at obscuring the facts.

Of all the acts of aggression between September and October 1970,
those steps taken with the intention of upsetting the Chilean economy
followed the most coherent plan and were carried out the most effectively. From mid-September on, these steps were accelerated, and, in a
way, they had the advantage of satisfying both the state of mind and
the concrete interests of the propertied class in Chile, besides following
their political wishes.

Yet neither the attempts to create economic chaos, nor the political
measures, nor the terrorist acts were successful. There were provocations and terrorist attempts to lure the Left into violence and give the
armed forces a chance to intervene; blandishments to some of the military; economic sabotage to break the will of the people; and finally, the
assassination of General Schneider. But none of these maneuvers succeeded in weakening the Left or provoking a military coup or a civil
war. In plenary session, Congress ratified Allende's election. The first
crisis was almost over. The umpteenth attempt of the year to change
the country's political system had once more failed.

Ambassador Korry was furious. Instead of getting back into favor
with the White House, he was confronted with a new fiasco. And to
make things even worse, Salvador Allende would take over the government at a time when the United States still had serious business pending

with Chile. This included the necessity of tearing down the Americans'
so-called meteorological stations and satellite tracing stations at various
points in Chilean territory — like Easter Island in the middle of the Pacific and Punta Arenas in the far South. Korry's indignation was two-fold;
it was also directed at Christian Democratic Minister of Foreign Affairs
Gabriel Valdés, then at the end of his career as chancellor after serving
in that post longer than any of his predecessors. Korry had never been
able to get along with him; there was no way to heal the breach then,
since it seems he had decided not to get along with Valdés even before
arriving in Chile, in reaction and in contrast to his predecessor, Ralph
Dungan. Valdés's independent actions had been an important factor
in Korry's failures.

And so it happened that while Valdés was being given a farewell party
by the foreign diplomatic corps, Korry disappeared from Santiago
without taking leave of anyone, and suddenly showed up beside a U. S.
military airplane on Easter Island, where he supervised the dismantling
of the U. S. installations and loading of the pieces into the plane.

The news of Korry's highly unusual behavior, which was an insult to
Chile and showed a lack of the most elementary courtesy, set off a
scandal. How this incident — which brought forth a strong official note
of protest to the United States — was experienced by Chileans is revealed in the following memo written by officials in the Foreign
Ministry for the foreign minister:

> As a consequence of the series of explosions set off by the French
> in the South Pacific, a question that preoccupied Chile's govern-
> ment as well as other South American governments on the Pacific
> coast (Chile sent France several notes of protest on the subject),
> the U. S. embassy in Santiago got in touch with the Chilean
> government, apparently offering to collaborate in measuring and
> controlling the atmospheric conditions on Easter Island.
>
> Those conversations gave rise to an official secret letter, dated
> March 24, 1966, from Ambassador Dungan to the foreign minister.
> (This letter was kept in the minister's files on the subject.) In
> short, it proposed that the governments of Chile and the United
> States agree to set up meteorological stations, for this and other
> related purposes, on Easter Island and eventually on Quinteros
> and Punta Arenas. Reference was made to the number and the
> status of the personnel required for them, etc. The letter, classi-
> fied as Top Secret, ended by saying that a reply would be con-
> sidered an acceptance and an official mutual agreement on the
> matter. There is no record in any file of the reply to Ambassador
> Dungan's note, but subsequent developments show that the em-

bassy as well as the government of the United States understood,
from a legal and diplomatic point of view, that the agreement be-
between the two governments had been concluded.

The clearest proof of this is the direct and concrete agreements
between the Chilean and the U. S. air forces, which came later,
regulating how the stations and material were to be set up and
operated; these agreements, mentioned in Ambassador Dungan's
initial communication, were legally binding arrangements which
grew out of the agreement between governments, and were subject
to their specifications. From what we know, they conformed to
the basic terms of the letter which needed only acknowledgment
from the receiver (no doubt this was done in writing, or at least
orally and officially) to close the agreement. Consequently, the
agreement existed at government level, since it was duly exe-
cuted. . . .

In any case, from an official standpoint there is no doubt that
in its confidential letter, the U. S. government formally stated that
it wanted the basic plan to set up and operate the stations, as
agreed upon by the two air forces, to be concluded at government
level. And, not having any proof that the Chilean government
did not want to do this, one must infer that the whole procedure
for the stations on Easter Island, Quinteros, and Punta Arenas was
the result of an agreement between the two governments, even if
we have no evidence of Chile's actual acceptance of the terms of
Ambassador Dungan's letter.

From a legal and diplomatic point of view, this is important
when we take into account the circumstances that surrounded
the dismantling of the stations on Easter Island, etc.

But before examining this situation, certain plausible theories
should be mentioned concerning how the station on Easter Island
may have served the United States.

As far as we know, American personnel were in direct and complete control of the administrative, scientific and technological
operation of the station. These personnel, who were rotated after
completing their duty, came mainly from the U. S. Defense Department, and consisted of civilians as well as military men. We
also know that other U. S. government agencies in charge of
scientific-military missions — including the Atomic Energy Commission, NASA, etc., as well as scientific groups of the academic
type like the National Science Foundation — have done work at
various times on this station. We also understand that at least
part of the equipment installed at the station was of a highly
"sophisticated" scientific nature, and was kept up to date with
the newest technological advances. At the same time, the periods
during which the station was operative for measuring the radio-

active contamination of the atmosphere became relatively shorter
from year to year, and depended on the number of explosions
set off annually by the French on Mururoa. We must also take
it for granted that the station was used by Americans and
Chileans for other meteorological services of a scientific and
practical nature. But there is no question that the type of equipment set up at the station, as well as the large number and quality
of its personnel, implied other objectives. We can only make a
conjecture about what was going on; for example, to check on
satellites of U. S. as well as other origin; to maintain communication with American reconnaissance flights in this and other
regions; to form part of a system for communication relays and
eventual refueling in case of war, etc. We must make it clear that
we have nothing substantial to back these conjectures, because,
as far as we know, neither the Chilean government nor the Air
Force was ever able to check up on these activities. On an international level in a speech to the United Nations General Assembly
in 1967, the Cuban foreign minister at least once called this
station (without naming it, but referring to Chile) a "North American military base."

. . . . The dismantling of the station on Easter Island was
done in the second half of October. The Air Force was told about
it (we do not know if it was informed by the U. S. Air Mission in
Chile or by those in charge of the station or in some other way).
The ministry, on the other hand, learned about it through a telephone call from the U. S. ambassador to the Chilean undersecretary
(Minister Valdés was then at the United Nations in New York), in
which he was briefly told, in an offhand manner, that the dismantling would take place. There was no written communication, and
apparently it was not specified how or exactly when it would be
done. Upset by the situation, which seemed to imply not only
that there would no longer be any meteorological service or any
station to measure atmospheric contamination, but also that this
development would greatly hamper, strategically and in other ways,
the operation of its own installations on Easter Island, the Chilean
Air Force approached the Ministry of Foreign Affairs with a
memorandum in which the effects of the U. S. decision to strip
the station on Easter Island, and subsequently on Quinteros and
Punta Arenas, were outlined.

Shortly after this, Minister Valdés learned from the commander
in chief of the Air Force, who had received the information directly from the commander on the island, that the Air Force was
deeply annoyed at the way the Easter Island station was being
stripped down, and also by the presence of Ambassador Korry, who,
it seemed, made a fast visit there expressly to supervise the op-

eration. Valdés also found out that American planes, brought
there for the purpose, were being used to carry away not just the
scientific and technological installations, but also adjoining ones —
even buildings made of light-weight material, bulldozers, and
other machinery that had been taken to the island to be used for
the work on the station; moreover, they were wasting no time
removing them. Other installations had been deliberately destroyed
without stopping to ask the Air Force (which apparently is the
usual procedure) if they wanted to buy the installations — both
the scientific equipment and the buildings — which theoretically
could have been used, at least in part, by the Air Force for some
of its meteorological work on the island.

On October 30, Minister Valdés sent a diplomatic note formally protesting to the U. S. ambassador and pointing out that
in stripping the station as they had done, they had not lived up
to the terms of their agreement that the Chilean government be
officially notified (the telephone call to the undersecretary about
the matter was not enough) and that, in any case, this procedure
violated international courtesy and could strain relations between
the two countries.

In the meantime, Ambassador Korry had made a statement to
the press, saying that he had gone to Easter Island to help distribute food parcels sent by the United States to the people on
the island. (It should be noted here that the station and the large
number of American personnel stationed there had two effects.
First, the Island's economic structure, the eating habits of its
people, the salary levels, employment, etc., were deeply affected.
Second, a stream of air traffic, more or less regular and frequent,
was set in motion by military planes from Panama and, perhaps,
from points in the United States. These facts should be kept in
mind, since the dismantling would leave in its wake a new and
serious distortion of the island's economic life, with all the consequences, including political ones, that implies.)

Ambassador Korry's statement provoked another response
from Minister Valdés in which he expressed his surprise at the
words and contents of the first.

But at the official diplomatic level, the U. S. embassy had received a note of protest. Ambassador Korry referred to it, trying
to answer its demands, in a letter he sent to Valdés on November
2, stating that there were no records in the U. S. embassy files
that connected this matter with any formal agreement between
governments, and including irrelevant comments about the mutual courtesy the two governments had shown in other dealings
shortly before this.

To conclude this account, Ambassador Korry had discussed this subject in a conversation with the Chilean government at that time, giving the following explanation: the budget had forced the U. S. government to terminate activities such as those at the weather station on Easter Island, Quinteros, and Punta Arenas; this decision had been made around the middle of the year. The Chilean Air Force had received a note explaining in detail how this was to be carried out, and the Ministry of Foreign Affairs had been verbally advised of it. They had rushed the stripping operation so that it would not be misinterpreted — which would have been the case if it had been done after the takeover by the new government — as a political move, when, in fact, it was nothing of the kind. Finally, his embassy carried no record in its files of an answer from the Government of Chile, sent from the Ministry of Foreign Affairs, on this subject, although he recognized that it was his predecessor who had handled the matter. Korry sounded a bit confused on this last point. What he had said contradicted the tenor of his letter to Minister Valdés, in which he seemed not to know of or even acknowledge the existence of the official secret communication from Ambassador Dungan, which contained the terms of the original agreement between the two governments.

Ambassador Korry's words were also answered verbally by the Chilean authorities: we had documents that disproved what he said; the political assessment of the right time to dismantle the bases was beside the point; moreover, this was a matter of international courtesy and the preservation of normal and correct relations between the U. S. embassy and the Chilean government; and, finally, the matter would be examined, in due time, by the Chilean Ministry of Foreign Affairs and the U. S. embassy. This ended the matter, for the time being, although Korry was obstinate on some of the points he had brought up.

Santiago, November 18, 1970

Note: Possible inexactitudes, omissions, or mistaken evaluations in the present memorandum are due to the fact that we had no written accounts of the situation.

It was during this serious incident, as clear an example as any both of Korry's attitude toward Chile and of the kind of instructions he received from his government, that Gabriel Valdés told the press, referring to the ambassador, "What Nature does not endow, diplomacy does not lend." It should be Edward Korry's epitaph. This was on November 3, the day of Allende's inauguration.

The president of the United States had not sent the usual congratulations. This was not only a break from tradition but, in the light of the historical significance of this type of message when a change of government takes place — and especially if it is a constitutional government as Allende's was — it was significant that the government of the United States should abstain from duly recognizing the new government.

At the very last moment, shortly before inauguration day, it was learned that the United States had decided to send Assistant Secretary of State for Latin America Charles Meyer as its official delegate to the inaugural ceremonies. The following memo, written for President Allende by Secretary Meyer's Chilean aide, summarizes the visit:

MEMORANDUM

Ref. Sojourn in Chile of the head of the special delegation from the United States to the transferal of power, Assistant Secretary of State Charles Meyer.

Assistant Secretary of State for Inter-American Affairs Charles Meyer arrived in Santiago on Sunday, November 1, and left on Thursday, the 5th.

His delegation consisted of Ambassador Korry, who was second in command, and John Fisher, the head of the State Department's Bureau of Andean and Pacific Affairs.

Mr. Meyer's career and personality

Secretary Meyer is a New England businessman, member of a Boston "Brahmin" family, coming from the upper class of a historically and culturally aware city, one of the most class-conscious in the United States. One of his ancestors was an admiral, and an ambassador to Rome and to imperial Russia. Charles Meyer has had a long career with Sears Roebuck, both within the United States and in Latin America. He lived for several years in Colombia as that firm's representative for the entire region. When he took over this position, he was in line to become president of that company, which has financial holdings considered very important among Americans. He is a relatively calm man, a Republican inside and out, capable of learning fast, but impressionable. He does not seem to have political ambitions. People who know him well, like Sol Linowitz, think that his actions and service in the State Department are guided by the desire to do a good job now and, immediately after that, become president of the firm he left. That would be one of the reasons for his tendency to adopt a moderate

tone in his position as a diplomat, to not aggravate potential conflicts with foreign governments; and that would also explain his
lack of aggressiveness in the permanent struggle for power between
the State Department and the White House. People in Washington
believe that he does not have a decisive influence on Nixon in
Latin American questions, but he has a reputation as a truthful
and tactful man. He is considered a man of good faith.

His activities in Chile

Meyer took part in all the official acts for the transferal of
power, except those taking place on Thursday, the day he left. He
did not seem to expect an interview with the president. He knew
how to cope outwardly with the tense situation between the
government and the U. S. embassy, but he did show a little ner-
vousness, which he held in check; this was apparent at his arrival
and in respect to his interview with the president of the Republic.
He bore up well, and even displayed a sense of humor, in the
expected tense atmosphere surrounding the American delegation
when it appeared in public, especially during the motorcades. He
reacted with composure to the few brief and halfhearted demonstrations against the United States. Once, hearing the shout "Chile
yes, Yankees no!" he stuck his head out the car window politely
and said in a normal voice, "Chile yes, Yankees yes," and then, as
he drew his head back in, he said in a low voice and with a scep-
tical smile, "Yankees maybe."

His appreciation of the inauguration ceremonies

It was obvious that he found the ceremony truly absorbing.
The well-mannered behavior of the people impressed him. The
crowd showed a certain amount of sympathy toward him, no
doubt in contrast to their feeling of contempt and indifference
toward Korry. Meyer sensed the profound significance behind the
ceremonies, and he understood well the respectfulness for our
institutions and their political symbolism — from the acts at the
plenary session of Congress to the Te Deum (which surprised him
as a significant act of spiritual acceptance of the new government
by the people), and the military parade, which he did not consider a mere show but a meaningful ceremony.

His impressions of the interview with the president

His interview with the president affected him more than any
of the other experiences. It proceeded with a seriousness and dignity that made a deep impression on him. Apparently he had not
expected the interview, or its tone or, perhaps, its content. On
this last point, however, he confided that, in Washington, he had

already imagined some of the things he was now hearing from
the president, meaning that he did not share and had never shared
any of the critical opinions of the press or, probably, of some sectors in the American government. From looking at him, and from
what is already known about him, one can tell that he will be an
honest reporter of what he has heard; in other words, he will not
let any preconceived notions or prejudices bias the impression
produced on him by the president's words. We must trust him
when he says that he will report the president's proposals directly
to Nixon. Later, he said privately that it was better to move his
departure up to Thursday the 5th, so that by Friday the 6th Nixon
would know all about this conversation. We can believe the sincerity of his opinion when he said that the interview had been
serious and friendly. In addition, shortly before leaving he told
his Chilean aide that he could tell the president, with all honesty
(this did not mean that it was a public message to President
Allende, who, after all, had called this interview something between him and Mr. Meyer), that he was very grateful for the opportunity to be present at the inauguration ceremonies, and especially
so for his interview with the president; and that this pointed to the
existence and continuity of good relations between the two
countries, which he considered fundamental. He ended by
saying that it was important to keep up these relations, whether
this was done at high or at low diplomatic levels, whether with
the foreign minister or directly with the president whenever he
deemed it necessary.

As Meyer was about to leave, talking in private about his interview with the president, this is how he summed up what he himself
had tried to say: First, he agreed completely with the president
that, in spite of their difference in size, population, etc., the dignity and the independence of the two countries deserved the same
respect. But we should remember that the contemporary world
demands that the relations between two countries depend not
only on direct and immediate two-way communication, but also
on multilateral encounters related to many lands and to problems
that concern the whole world. Consequently, the respect for the
dignity, independence, and interests of each of the two countries
is necessary in all areas and aspects of international life where
both countries are present. Second, regarding the situation of
credits to Chile, he wanted to point out that for a long time he
had shared the feelings of his government that bilateral economic
cooperation should be replaced by a system that would channel
such activities through international financial agencies, as he had
explained to ex-Minister Zaldivar about a year and a half before
(probably at the meeting of IDB governors in Guatemala in
1969). This line of action depoliticized the economic-financial

relations of the United States with underdeveloped countries, and —for this as well as other reasons — the United States thought that this line conformed more to the will of such countries to strengthen their independence and insure that their dignity was respected.

In other private conversations related to this subject, Mr. Meyer stressed the need for each country to have a thorough understanding of what the other believes its legitimate prestige to be, as a nation and in the presence of its leaders. In this connection, he thought that the personality of each country and the opportunity their diplomats had of knowing each other's countries were essential.

Perhaps what impressed Mr. Meyer most during his conversation with President Allende was his personality, seriousness, national spirit, and integrity. He emphasized this more than once in private conversations, repeating, each time, that he had imagined him this way before coming to Chile. He didn't come right out with an opinion about the Popular Unity parties and movements, since his sense of elementary courtesy probably told him that he would be speaking out of turn. However, it is safe to suppose that, taken together, his experiences during his short stay in Chile made him form impressions, founded on firsthand experience, that were much more reasonable than those held by the usual Washington official. And yet, on one occasion (this is something he probably got from Korry) he expressed, in a vague way, his concern about the people (not named or identified by him) whom the president had "around" him. His Chilean aide-de-camp immediately told him that those suspicions were irrational; that he ought to reject any suspicions and ridiculous ideas about the way decisions were made in the Chilean government. After all, in the United States people thought it was silly the way foreigners believed that all political, economic, commercial, and financial decisions, as well as those on national security, were the product of a kind of mysterious "big brain," which always acts with aggressive intentions, never making errors, and which is also the leader of a plot against the interests of the rest of the world. Chile, he pointed out, has an institutional regime that answers to the people, since the people run it, and is a true democracy. Mr. Meyer seemed to accept these words in good faith and sincerity. As he was saying goodbye, he told his Chilean aide-de-camp, with some emotion, that the human beings who make up a nation are the same the world over and that the confidence and hope we can have in countries where the people govern made him want to ask God's blessing for the peoples of Chile and the United States.

Santiago, November 6, 1970

In this acount, the interview of President Allende with Charles Meyer and Edward Korry stands out. This was the president's first meeting with an official representative of a foreign country. It was on this occasion that Salvador Allende addressed the assistant secretary of state for Latin America with these words, "Mr. Meyer, I am not someone just off the boat[2] in the history of Chile . . . ."

A confidential memorandum prepared as the official account of the interview, and dated November 4, gives a detailed report of it.

On November 4, 1970, His Excellency the President of the Republic gave audience to the assistant secretary of state and head of the United States delegation to the presidential turning over of office, Mr. Charles Meyer. His Excellency was accompanied by the Minister of Foreign Affairs, Clodomiro Almeyda, and by Ramón Huidobro. Mr. Meyer was accompanied by the United States' ambassador to Chile, Mr. Edward Korry. Armando Uribe was also present. The audience lasted thirty-five minutes. His Excellency opened the interview by expressing his pleasure that Mr. Meyer had come to Chile as the bearer of President Nixon's personal congratulations to the president of Chile, adding that this was the first audience he was holding — something quite significant. The president of Chile was satisfied to start official exchanges with the United States in this manner. But even before the plenary session of Congress, he had already seen to it that a personal representative of the highest level, the distinguished Senator Hugo Miranda of the Radical party (a party that has been active in Chilean politics for one hundred and ten years), had contacted the ambassador of the United States in order to prepare the way for these exchanges, indicating his government's intentions and his desire to have the best possible relations with the United States and to receive from that government due respect for Chile.

Chile, the president said, is a small country, and the United States is a world power. However, each of them has absolutely the same right to dignity and proper consideration for its respective national interests. Chile and its government would like to have the best relations with the United States. Those relations go back a very long time, they have naturally had their ups and downs, and yet they have been maintained without interruption. This must continue.

Its history and the recent election of the Popular Government show that Chile is a unique country. This is something Mr. Meyer can see at firsthand by his present visit. As for the president, the election of the Popular Government, his own political life, spanning more than thirty years in the Chilean Congress (which is a

Parliament with more than one hundred and fifty years of
uninterrupted republican life behind it), and his personal participation in the cabinet of President Aguirre Cerda's Popular Front
government (one of the three examples of a Popular Front coali-
tion government in the world) make him an authority on Chile's
special character. Our country will be independent and freedom
will reign. Freedom of the press in Chile will allow the expression
of opinions that the United States may consider critical of it, and
our government will not be able to stop them. Besides, the same
thing occurs in the United States, where the press is also free and
prints far-reaching and unjust criticism of the people, the country, and the governing heads of foreign nations. This has been the
experience of the president himself, before and after his election.
And so the only way for the governments of the two countries not
to commit errors or have misunderstandings in their appreciation
of each other is, first of all, to rely on the deeds and the actions of
each government. We will be known by our acts and only by our
acts. And secondly, Chile's attitude toward the United States can
only be known and judged by texts officially authorized by the
government of Chile.

Assistant Secretary of State Meyer, who listened to all this
with profound and friendly interest, assented with a nod, saying,
"Yes, Mr. President."

The President continued: I am very satisfied with President
Nixon's speech before the United Nations, especially when he
spoke of the right of the people to self-determination, and of the
principle of nonintervention. Chile is independent, free, and sovereign, and its foreign policy is based on these principles. But I
want to emphasize that there are many forms of pressure. I don't
believe, I can never believe, that the existence of a popular government in Chile can affect its foreign credit rating in the United
States.

At this point, Assistant Secretary Meyer interrupted to say that
he was a firm promoter of the multilateral policy of economic aid
which the United States was putting into effect. This meant that
there would not be a flow of credits of a bilateral nature, as in the
past; and this change could already be seen in the last few years.
But this multilateral policy, according to the U. S. government,
benefits, economically and politically, those countries that receive
credits as well as the United States, and is better suited to the
sovereign independence of those nations that need credits.

The President then explained that, in keeping with the Popular
Unity's program, which his government would put into effect,
Chile's economy would be divided into three sectors: the public
sector, which would include copper, iron, nitrate, and resources

and raw materials basic to Chile's economy; the mixed sector, with the participation of the state; and the private sector. This division has existed in Chile for a long time and will continue to exist. In this sense, the government will not be (as those people say, who don't know or don't want to know) a communist, socialist, Marxist or whatever kind of government those people call it. It will be a people's government that is carrying out a public program with its own Chilean characteristics, which respectable and traditional forces in Chilean politics, ranging from Marxists to Christians, have agreed to support. It will be a Chilean government, an authentic national experience, as others before it have been, like the Popular Front. For this very reason, no one can believe or say that the government of Chile will export Popular Unity to other Latin American countries. To export Popular Unity, the Chilean formula, it would have to export democracy first! And Mr. Meyer well knows that this isn't easy at all, where Latin American countries are concerned. The United States has had this experience.

What we are going to do in Chile is something like what has been done in the United States; we will develop the country, give equal opportunities to all men, in the broadest meaning of the word, to those I have called the "human couple," so that each and every Chilean will have dignity, real freedom, and a just and human life. That is what the United States has done, and it can therefore understand Chile's wish to do the same thing. A few minutes away from this presidential residence there are Chileans who live and die in conditions that are inhuman. This is going to stop. To do it we will take steps already taken by the United States, where, for example, you have laws against monopolies, where President Kennedy, I remember, stood up to the private interests of the steel industry in order to defend the general interests of the country. We will do it within the law and according to the Constitution. We will modify the law and the Constitution, if necessary, but that modification will be done, as it always has been done in Chile, according to the laws and the Constitution now in force. Mr. Meyer and the United States government have been able to verify that this is how political and economic processes are carried out in Chile. Popular Unity's rise to power proves this beyond a doubt.

We shall start the nationalization of foreign interests, including the American ones, in order to bring over to the public sector those goods that belong and must belong to the entire country. We will do it in accordance with Chilean law, with all the respect that this implies for those interests and for the recognition of our rights. But we shall treat American interests in the same way we treat Chilean interests. These measures will not be directed against the United States, because they will be measures legally taken in

sectors where there will be no discrimination against those interests because of their origin, but only insofar as they affect the
legitimate interests of the country. Measures will be taken without
distinguishing between private foreign and private Chilean investments. All will strictly conform to the existing law or to that
passed by Congress.

The corresponding indemnifications are something that will be
discussed with the firms that own the nationalized goods, not
with the government of the country of these firms; their respective investments and the way in which those private companies
were established in Chile presupposed an exclusive relationship
between private individuals and the government of Chile. The
Chilean law courts, a state power that is independent of the Executive, are a permanent guarantee that the question will be resolved
according to the law.

It will be done this way, in accordance with Chile's traditional
institutions. No comparisons can be made with nationalizations
in other countries where there has been neither longstanding
democracy nor responsible institutions and authorities, like those
Chile has known throughout its history — countries that passed
abruptly from one historical stage to another. This cannot be
applied to Chile and its government, as Mr. Meyer has seen and
can still see.

Mr. Meyer had been listening very attentively to what was being
said.

There is something else I would like to point out, the President
continued. Chile has never allowed, nor will it now, any country
to set up within its boundaries military or any other kind of bases
that would interfere with the country's sovereignty. Never.
Whatever happens, under my government Chile's sovereignty and
independence will be safeguarded and protected from any foreign
power.

Our relations with the United States will be those that exist
between two independent and sovereign countries. There may
be differences of opinion between us in the United Nations. On
some questions Chile will side with the United States, on others
it will vote with the nonaligned countries, and on still others, with
the Soviet Union and the socialist countries. But there can only
be friendly relations between sovereign nations when they fully
acknowledge that their interests are not necessarily identical, and
have a clear idea of what points they agree on, and where their
national interests differ. Respect for each other's position on
specific points of divergence is the very basis of international relations. It is the only way that each can keep its national dignity.
No relationship is possible unless the dignity of each is recognized.

Thus, the United States must be aware that Chile's stand on international issues will depend exclusively and absolutely on its national interests, just as we have understood that the United States acts in the interest of its own national well-being. In this respect, the United States must know that its security, which we realize is a fundamental motive behind its foreign policy positions, will never be endangered by Chile or by anything that happens there. We are as interested in Chile's security as the United States is interested in its own, and the two interests do not conflict. The defense of Chile's security will never endanger the security of the United States.

Mr. Meyer agreed strongly on this point.

Ambassador Korry interrupted to say that they were aware that the concept of national dignity implied a mutual cultural understanding; each of the two countries — in this case Chile and the United States — must understand exactly what the other conceives as its own dignity. And, for this, adequate communication between the two countries is essential.

The President used this last remark to say: That is exactly why I want to tell you, Mr. Meyer, that what happened on Easter Island in the last few days has created a situation that affects Chile's dignity as well as its interests. The Air Force is deeply annoyed at the way the stations on the island were dismantled. That was neither the way nor the moment to do it. There is nothing friendly about this action.

Assistant Secretary of State Meyer said that he realized that this had caused economic problems for the people on the island, but that this kind of effect could be corrected.

The President interrupted him to explain that it was not an economic problem, but something different and more serious. These actions had been carried out by the American representatives in a way that affected the dignity and respect that Chile, and specifically its Air Force on Easter Island, deserved.

Ambassador Korry observed that the dismantling of the stations was something that had been brought on by the reduction of the U. S. budget for such installations. In short, it had been a decision that had nothing to do with the relations between the two countries. In making the decision for the dismantling, the embassy had found itself in a dilemma: whether to carry it out before or after the new government took power. If they did it after the transferal of office, it could be misinterpreted as an unfriendly act. And so they had thought it would be better to do it before, in spite of the little time they had left. Under these circumstances, and since Foreign Minister Valdés was then at the United Nations,

Ambassador Korry had telephoned the undersecretary to tell him that the stations would be stripped down. There had been no need for any other formality because the agreement on this had been made between the air forces of the two countries, and not between their governments.

No, Mr. Ambassador, the President exclaimed. There is a written agreement showing that this is a question between the two governments, and not simply between the two air forces. The minister of foreign affairs has the document in question.

Ambassador Korry muttered that they had nothing to prove that such an agreement had been made. Perhaps Ambassador Dungan, his predecessor, had made it, but they had no written record of it.

The President gave Minister Almeyda a chance to speak. He said: I have the official note from the ambassador of the United States stating that it is an agreement between governments.

Minister Almeyda started to take the document out of his portfolio to read it.

Seeing that Ambassador Korry looked ready to begin a discussion on this point, the President broke in to say: There's no need for that now. But I want to insist that there was no reason to rush into the operation in order to get it done before the present government assumed power. If the United States had expressed its intention to end the agreement and Chile had had no objection, my government would have accepted that, and would have explained to the people that this was in Chile's best interest. There was, and there still is, no reason why questions of mutual interest, like this, cannot be properly discussed by Chile, through its foreign minister, and the embassy of the United States. It is the only way for two countries with normal relations between them to communicate. Haste and unilateral action are not the way.

With these words, the President rose. He considered the session ended.

Assistant Secretary Meyer then said: I have listened with great interest to everything that has been said, and I want to thank you for this interview. I am leaving Chile on Thursday because I can't get a flight for Friday, and so I will not be able to attend the reception on Thursday. I'm very sorry about this, because I am very fond of Chile, and this fondness goes well beyond my duties here now, Mr. President. I am fond of Chile because I understand very well that it is a country different from any other in Latin America or the rest of the world — a country that deserves everyone's respect for the way in which it conducts its policies and for it its people, beginning with its leaders. I will take your words to President Nixon, and I will report them faithfully.

Assistant Secretary Meyer and Ambassador Korry left the
President's office at 10:05.

Santiago, November 4, 1970

While this was taking place in Santiago and Assistant Secretary Meyer
himself seemed convinced of the evident political sincerity of Salvador
Allende and the Chilean Government, in Washington the National Security Council was deciding to apply the policy of the big stick against
Chile.

7

Assistant Secretary of State Meyer's short stay in Chile had been dramatic for him and Ambassador Korry. Behind their diplomatic masks, a tension had been growing between them: each represented, on a reduced scale, the division of opinion between the State Department and the White House, which was becoming more pronounced in Washington in early November. It was common knowledge that, after the uproar caused in 1970 by Korry's Report on Foreign Aid and after what happened in Chile, Secretary of State Rogers and Assistant Secretary Meyer saw Korry's behavior as the most ruthless example of what they were up against in the political and bureaucratic struggle with the international apparatus set up by Kissinger in the White House. Even ITT's field reporters, Hendrix and Berrelez, who had not run into this type of situation before they began their secret activities in Chile, as well as the ITT directors in the United States, saw, within a few days, exactly what was happening. ITT's secret memos are filled with statements like this: "The rift between Ambassador Ed Korry and his superior at the State Department has reached the point where he deals now directly with the White House and does not always share his input and instructions with State." The same October 21 memo also stated that Korry's colleagues were saying that Charles Meyer was determined to get him out of Chile and, if possible, out of the State Department.

Who was Korry? A Chilean report of 1970, written for Minister Valdés, describes Korry as the typical American proconsul:

81

Edward Korry is a journalist by profession. He worked for a
long time at UPI, lived, among other places, in Yugoslavia and
France, and was the news agency's director in several European
capitals. He was called to Washington by President Kennedy, who
had decided to look for people outside the State Department and
active politics to fill ambassadorial posts, especially in Africa.
Thus, he appointed Korry ambassador to Ethiopia, just as he had
already given similar appointments to people from the universities
like Professor Gullion, assigned at the time to the Kinshasa Congo,
and today at the Fletcher School of Law and Diplomacy. Korry
filled the post in Ethiopia for several years. He had a tendency to
deal directly with the Emperor who, they say, finally had personal
problems with the ambassador because of his proconsular behavior.

Perhaps the most outstanding thing about his assignment in
Ethiopia was an undertaking he directed, with the collaboration of
other U. S. ambassadors and officials in Africa, to work out a complete report on what U. S. policy in that region should be. Korry
was so active in putting this together that it became known as the
Korry Report on Africa. The report was not implemented by the
State Department, its ideas were not tried out, and the Johnson
administration forgot all about it. In spite of this, or perhaps for
this very reason, the Korry Report had great success in specialized
circles. Recent books on Africa reserve a high place for it, probably because the United States has never had a coherent policy on
that continent; consequently, the report appears to be an authority
on what should have been done.

During his mission in Ethiopia, Korry received Nixon — then a
private citizen — who stayed with him as his guest. They had long
conversations. This is important and will be discussed later. When
Ambassador Dungan left Santiago, Korry was called to replace him.
During the Kennedy administration, Korry was considered a Democrat, although he does not seem to have actually been a member
of that party. Before going to Santiago, he had already decided
that he would run the embassy in a manner very different from
Dungan's. Although these two men were on friendly terms, they
did not seem to have the same psychological or political outlook.
Korry maintained that he had been instructed to change the embassy's style completely, to stay out of Chilean political activities,
and to keep away from political figures in the government or in
the opposition. When President Nixon was elected, the normal
thing would have been for Korry, who was not a career man, to
leave the embassy and return to private life. We know that by
April 1969, he had already been notified that he would soon be
replaced, and the name of his successor, a man from the State
Department, was already known. Korry got ready to return to the

United States, as he said, to "look for work." But he used this occasion to pull two tricks out of the bag like those he would use later on.

First, he made the most of some declarations by a Chilean senator, in early May, to attack the government of Chile violently and to make it appear to the executive branch and the U. S. Senate that he was an ambassador who was being persecuted and criticized only because he defended the prestige of the United States. (That is how he put the matter to the State Department, which backed him with an official statement, and to the Senate, which saw him in a secret session of the Foreign Relations Committee, where he was equally defended.)

Secondly, using the friendship he had struck up with Nixon in Ethiopia, Korry sent him a personal letter reminding the President that in a conversation some years back in Addis Ababa, he had told him that if he were elected president, he would need people like Korry for key countries outside of the big powers. Korry was kept on the job, although they had already been preparing his successor in Chile.

This produced some bad feelings in the State Department, and confirmed Korry's ties with the White House and the international policy team that works there and which has wider powers than its competitor. All of this — his prestige as author of the Korry Report on Africa, his personal reputation as ambassador (he was then the only ambassador named by Kennedy who continued in that post) — persuaded the State Department to ask him, in the second half of 1969, to coordinate its program for a new foreign aid policy. This job was proposed to him by the department itself as a reply to the special commission that President Nixon had created to study the same subject. From all indications, this Commission would come to the conclusion that everything connected with the international economic cooperation of the United States should be taken from the State Department (where it functions today as AID); this would greatly cut the State Department's power in international affairs. Korry, who was aware of the struggle between the White House and State Department teams, accepted the job, and took it on almost single-handedly. He prepared a report that was very critical of AID, along the same lines he believed would be followed by Nixon's special Commission, which was headed by an expert, Peter Peterson. The secretary of state turned down Korry's report and asked him to amend it. Knowing Peterson's work much better by then, Korry fixed up his report to look even more like the Commission's. He turned it in to the secretary of state, who became furious and had it filed away. Korry was all set for this move. He simultaneously got in touch with friends at

the *New York Times* and other American newspapers and press
agencies (as a former journalist he has many such connections) and
at the White House. And, one day before Peterson's report was to
come out, he had large sections of his own report, which closely
resembled Peterson's, given outstanding coverage by the news
media. This insured his unpopularity with the State Department,
and he went over to the side of the White House's international
team.

This is why, in the eyes of President Nixon and his White House
staff, Korry was the best U. S. ambassador in Latin America. In
Washington, people were saying that his opinions carried more
weight in the White House than those of the assistant secretary for
Latin America, Charles Meyer.

Korry's attitude before the presidential elections in Chile seems
to have been this: he was convinced that Alessandri would win,
fearful of Popular Unity's chances in the elections, and careful to
avoid doing anything that would make people say that he was
meddling in Chilean politics. After the elections, his reaction
seems to have been to send reports to the United States that were
very critical of the future of the Popular Unity government, and
to declare that it was provoking a series of grave situations against
which, as far as he could see, nothing could be done. His next
strategy, still in progress, seems to be to stir up friction and confrontations that will provoke aggressive response, so that he can
appear to the Executive and to Congress as a victim of his bold
defense of U. S. interests and its reputation, which is being subjected to attacks that only he can confront. In the event of a future
situation of this kind, he would have two alternatives: to attack
and counterattack in such a way as to make the United States quickly step in and insist that he be kept on as ambassador, since anything else would be a display of weakness before the Chilean government; or else, to provoke the latter into declaring him *persona non
grata*, which, with the Chilean situation as it is now, would probably add merit to his name and place him in a position to obtain
other official positions in the United States.

He is a tremendous egotist who obviously has ambitions to play
a larger role in diplomatic as well as political life. He can't keep
his mouth shut in public or in private, and talks for hours on end.

He puts on a show of courage when he does something bold or
when he acts and talks insolently, but he probably suffers from
moral cowardice. In spite of appearances, his violent outbursts,
his poor manners, his rudeness, and his provocations are never
entirely gratuitous; that is, he is capable of rationalizing what he
does and making the most of it. He always acts with one eye on
the U. S. government and the news media; their reactions have a

lot to do with his own actions. He affects a snobbish air, combined with a certain contempt, and tries to use the storehouse of
knowledge and facts he acquired as a newspaperman to pass for a
cultured man. He cannot hide the irritation produced in him by
Chile as a country and as a human community with its own history. Thus, the resentment he seems to feel toward Popular
Unity's victory is turned against the country that allowed it.
His personality inspires terror mixed with admiration in those
who work under him at the embassy and in people in the State
Department. Very few persons are totally devoted to him. Most
people admire his capacity for work and his dynamism, but do
not seem to be personally drawn to him.

    He is not very loyal to those who work with him. In Washing-
ton, those in high political places regard him with some irony.
They see through his egotism and have little confidence in his
judgment; but what protects Edward Korry is his cunning, his
bureaucratic maneuvering, his ability to sense where the real
centers of power lie, his political versatility, his easy access to
the universities and top academic circles, and, above all perhaps,
his superior talents when measured against the mediocrity of
those American bureaucrats actually concerned with Latin
America.

Korry's outbursts, so familiar to everyone in Washington and Santiago,
erupted often during Meyer's visit to Chile; the Chileans who accompanied him saw, on more than one occasion, the efforts Meyer made to
contain himself and the difficult time Korry's wife had calming down
the volatile ambassador. Meyer was in Santiago for the inauguration
when he learned that American policy toward Chile was definitely being
decided in the National Security Council in Washington. Those were
decisive days. Korry continued to recommend a tougher line of action
to the White House. Meyer believed he could suggest a more flexible
alternative, with the same objectives in sight — since there was no ques-
tioning American policy toward Popular Unity and Allende — that
would use other means with greater scope. For the State Department
this other attitude would be more effective.

    The personal and political differences between Korry and Meyer
were clear. Korry probably hampered Meyer's actions in Santiago, or
perhaps Meyer felt his way blocked, vis à vis his government, by his
disagreements with the ambassador. Anyway, on the fourth, when
Meyer realized that the National Security Council had set a definite
policy which did not fall into line with the vision he had acquired since
his arrival in Chile, he became visibly anxious to get back to Washington

as soon as possible. He had decided to go straight to the National Security Council, presided over by Nixon himself, with his differing opinion, to present the contradictions in the official stands of the State
Department and the White House. He asked for a hearing in Washington
as soon as possible. On the afternoon of November 4, the same day he
saw Allende, he told his Chilean aide-de-camp that he had to move up
his return trip to Thursday the fifth so that he could let President Nixon
know what President Allende had said the moment he arrived in Washington. He asked to be excused from attending any more receptions or
interviews, and flew back.

The plan of action of the policy makers closest to the Executive and
the White House team headed by Henry Kissinger, which supported
adopting a stiffer policy toward Allende's government as soon as it
assumed power, had been in the making since October, when they
realized how difficult it would be to stop Popular Unity from taking
office, no matter what economic sabotage or political aggression the
United States used. Vice-President Merriam of ITT heard this on October 9 from William Broe of the CIA and rushed the news to John
McCone, director of ITT and ex-director of the CIA: "I was rather
surprised to learn that in this man's opinion the Nixon Administration
will take a very, very hard line when and if Allende is elected. As soon
as expropriations take place, and providing adequate compensation is
not forthcoming, he believes that all sources of American monetary
help, either through aid or through the lending agencies here in Washington, will be cut off. He assures me that the President has taken at
this time (better late than never, I guess) a long, hard look at the situation and is prepared to move after the fact."[1]

We can point to November 6 as the approximate date on which the
final draft of the policy on Chile, discussed a few days before by the
National Security Council, was adopted in Washington; a decision
probably made under the supervision of Nixon and Kissinger, with
Rogers, Meyer, and others present. We must stress the fact that this
decision cannot be considered more or less "benevolent" than other
possibilities; it was, in fact, a decision to strangle Chile gradually. And
it gave Washington the advantage of leaving the way open for future
options that could supplement or substitute for it later on. Kissinger
must have been won over to this policy by the possibilities it offered
for escalation, and the latitude it left the American government to
intensify gradually its pressures on Chile through economic, financial,
and political interference or armed intervention. Action could be
taken against Chile in different parts of the world, in countries that

were in the American system in Europe, Latin America, etc. The
United States could hold Chile up as an example to the Soviet Union to
show the extent of its global power, joining U. S. government interests
with those of multinational consortiums and large capital investment
companies. All this would take from one to three years, the time
Kissinger needed to carry out his grand design of global strategy destined to create a new international order, one which would be favorable
to the American system.

This policy would "globalize" Chile's case. American actions and
inactions in Chile could be used by the United States to score points
against the Soviet Union, China, Western Europe and Japan, as well as
the Third World. It would — and this must have pleased Kissinger —
apply what David Landau, in his book *Kissinger: The Uses of Power*,
calls the most characteristic instrument of Nixon-Kissinger policy:
the concept of "linkage." According to this concept, all points of
conflict in the world exist in a single continuum which connects the
Soviet Union and the United States. In this context, Landau points out,
the solution of concrete problems depends less on the merits of each
specific case than on the balance of world power between the two
parties; the supposition behind this "linkage" is that the solution of a
major crisis anywhere in the world can be predetermined by the degree
of strength and stability that one or both of the opponents have shown
in other zones.

Chile, then, was to be totally absorbed into the United States' grand
design for a new world order. To utilize Chile as a helpful and dynamic
element, it was in U. S. interests to give the Allende government a little
time. Meanwhile, the United States would gradually sap its strength,
thus offering France, Italy, and other industrialized countries and
democracies that did not want to play ball, a test case taken from real
life (or a *corpus vile*, if you prefer) of the series of consequences and
the final disaster awaiting those who disrupt the system.

As the United States saw it, the Chilean disaster, the coup d'etat,
civil war and fascism were only in suspension, and would come in good
time to serve the needs of American world policy.

One might object that this is an overestimation of the capacity and
power of American imperialism and does not take into account the importance of internal conflicts inherent in a country like Chile. On the
contrary, in American strategy, the conflicts within a national society
become international factors for political manipulation. When the
center of power of the imperialist system adopts a basic political program, as in Chile's case in 1970, and considers the use of each and

every means in its power, including military force, the internal political
life of the country in question can no longer be distinguished from international politics. The country can of course defend itself against
imperialism and be victorious, but the struggle would be difficult, long,
and uncertain. In cases like this, bloody incidents multiply, and the
most violent actions, apparently internal — like the military coup in
September 1973 — are mere episodes in the fight against imperialism.

The Chile policy formulated in November 1970 by Nixon and Kissinger
contained all the contingent hypotheses and plans that the United
States' center for foreign intervention had worked out, including, of
course, the Pentagon's 1970 plan, the first effects of which were witnessed in the "Navy Band" incident. They would also use all the measures planned and applied between September and October of that year,
according to the project revealed by the CIA on September 29. They
would apply the specific suggestions made by ITT during those months,
especially those contained in reports from Gerrity to President Geneen
on October 20, to ex-Director of the CIA McCone on the twenty-first,
and on October 23, from ITT's Vice-President Merriam to Dr. Henry
Kissinger — who thanked him on November 9, as we have already seen,
saying that the White House would certainly keep in mind these ideas
and suggestions. (Kissinger was simply reflecting the decision adopted a
few days before by the National Security Council.) They would take
advantage of the entente among various American corporations (Anaconda, Kennecott, ITT, banks, etc.) which got together in early 1971
and agreed to pressure Chile,[2] and the ensuing actions of those companies — for example, Kennecott's embargoes on copper. They would
block international credits accorded to Chile, not only those granted by
American organizations like Eximbank (this was publicly announced in
mid-1971) but also those of international organizations like the IDB or
the World Bank (which declared Chile a grave credit risk at the end of
1970) and other American and European private financing agencies.
They would pressure countries in Europe and the rest of the world not
to invest in Chile, as Arnold Nachmanoff, who was in charge of Latin
America on Kissinger's team, assured ITT at the beginning of 1971.[3]
They would make it as difficult as possible for other countries to grant
Chile credit or to trade with it. When the time came, they would
block the renegotiation of Chile's enormous foreign debt, isolating
those creditors inclined to grant Chile credit and cutting down Chile's
chances for international negotiation in this field as much as possible.
They would stop (Chile was to go through this painful experience)

the supplies of spare parts, machinery, and installations, as well as the renovation of industries and all technological development. They would try to paralyze transportation more and more: in the air, by preventing the purchase of airplanes; at sea, by maneuvering its control of merchant fleets in maritime conferences; by rail, by interrupting the renovation of equipment; and, finally, on the roads, by cutting off the shipment of spare parts. They would force down the price of copper and distort the international market. (There are many indications and proofs of this since the end of 1970; one of the latest initiatives of this kind was President Nixon's announcement in March 1973 that the large stock of U. S. copper reserves would be put on the market.) They would support all the actions of groups opposing Popular Unity by introducing clandestine dollars into Chile, thus provoking serious distortions in Chile's monetary system and uncontrollable inflationary pressures. (This was notorious both during the truckowners' and shopkeepers' strike in October 1972, when the value of the dollar suffered a steep drop on the black market because of the secret dollar influx, and after April 1973, during the series of trade-union strikes.) They would also cooperate with these groups through other acts or refrainments. And finally, they would maintain and even increase the supply (this began with the Navy and later extended to all branches of the armed forces) of military equipment and armaments under commercially attractive conditions, in an attempt to deepen their institutional contact with these forces.

Most of these actions, effectively applied by the United States after November 1970 (and this is only a partial list), can be reduced to a single plan to strangle Chile's economy. With this as a pretext, strictly political measures were also carried out, both internationally and within the country, some openly, but most of them secretly.

When President Allende spoke of the invisible blockade which Chile was subjected to by imperialist action, and when, in his United Nations speech in 1972, he quoted Neruda's phrase, "Chile is a silent Vietnam," he was only speaking of economic measures like those I have listed. When he also denounced the underhanded aggressiveness of ITT and the multinational companies, he did not accuse the United States itself of directing this policy of intervention. It was only on April 10, 1973, in his speech before the Assembly of World Labor Unions in Santiago, that he publicly revealed the immediate links between ITT's subversive acts and the U. S. government. These ties had already been proven beyond a doubt at Senator Church's hearings in Washington a few days before.

Now, however, it is possible to judge the full extent of the U. S.

government's systematic action; it applied its policy to destroy deliberately, on every level — beginning with the economy and going as far as military subversion — Salvador Allende's government, Popular Unity, the Chilean state, and the popular movement. As soon as this American policy was seen in its true form of economic aggression, it was given the name "the ripe pear" in Chile. The United States lay low, waiting for the fruit of the Chilean experience to ripen, forcing it to mature with its acts of aggression so that it would eventually rot, and Allende's regime would come crashing down. This intention was obvious from the American acts of aggression, public and private, which sought — as the Spanish saying goes — *harcerlo madurar a palos* ("to ripen it by beating it with a stick").

Shortly after the Allende administration took over, the United States solemnly sent its first official warnings.

On December 30, 1970, Nixon received the Chilean ambassador to Washington and gave him a message for his president. Richard Nixon was accompanied by General Haig — at that time Kissinger's deputy and later Nixon's chief assistant. The particulars of how this interview came to be arranged shed such light on Dr. Kissinger's influence in the White House and the administration that they were quoted, as an example of his power, in the United States (in articles in the *New York Times* and the *Washington Post*) and in France (in an analysis of Kissinger made by Oliver Todd in *Le Nouvel Observateur*). When the Chilean ambassador complained to Kissinger that the State Department would not give him the interview, he was told that that was natural for he had knocked at the wrong door. And Kissinger arranged the interview right away.

The text of the confidential report sent by the ambassador to President Allende (from Foreign Minister Almeyda's files) follows:

Strictly confidential.

Interview with Nixon

1. In early December I had an interview with Charles Meyer in order to:
    a. inform him officially that my mission in Washington would end in December

  b. ask for appointments with President Nixon and Secretary
  of State Rogers so that I might say goodbye to them.
 Furthermore, I said I wished to visit him again before I left, adding that I would like to see him with his whole staff.

 2. Two weeks later, after many calls from the embassy about
this (during that time I had been away from Washington on a conference tour of universities, local committees of the Council on
Foreign Relations, and groups from the Chilean colony), Meyer's
office informed me that the interviews with Secretary of State
Rogers and with Meyer and his staff had been arranged but that it
was impossible for me to see Nixon. He didn't have time to receive
me! (I had only asked for a five minute audience.)

 3. At the end of my interview with Meyer and his staff, I asked
to see him alone for a few minutes. I told him that I was leaving
the United States very annoyed because the President would not
receive me. That this was not only an act of discourtesy, but a
political error as well. That this action evidently would not help
to maintain the good relations between the two governments, which
the secretary of state said he favored. That I would have to explain
what had happened — adding my own views — not only to my
government, but, eventually, in public also. That this would oblige
the President of Chile, for simple reasons of reciprocity, to turn
down an interview with Ambassador Korry, who would soon have
to take his leave (this was a foregone conclusion). Obviously upset, Meyer asked me not to say anything yet to the Chilean government, and said that he would personally see what he could do. I
agreed to his request.

 4. Two days later, when I went to the State Department for
my interview with Secretary of State Rogers, I was told by Mr.
John Fisher, "country director" for Chile, that Assistant Secretary
Meyer (who was then away on Christmas vacation) had asked him
to tell me that, unfortunately, Meyer had not been able to change
Nixon's decision not to see me.

 5. Consequently, at the end of my interview with Secretary
Rogers (and to the amazement of Fisher, who was present), I
repeated even more bluntly my profound annoyance at President
Nixon's refusal to receive me. Like Meyer, the Secretary was upset
and promised to see what could be done.

 6. Neither Meyer, nor Rogers later on, tried to explain this
refusal by the fact (which is true) that it is not customary for
ambassadors to take leave of the President. (This seems reasonable
to me, considering the size of the diplomatic corps in Washington,
its constant turnover, and the many obligations of the President
of the United States.) They both spoke of the President's over-
whelming work. In his eagerness to defend him, Rogers told me

that even the cabinet members themselves had great difficulty getting in to see him. He probably saw the look of surprise on my face, because he added that fortunately, he was one of the privileged few among the cabinet members who could talk to the President any time he needed to.

7. A day or so later, I was told that Rogers was very sorry that he had not been able to get me the interview with the President. Once more, this information was accompanied by the request not to interpret this as a political act; the President simply could not find time for the interview.

8. Applying the wise maxim "Be one and a half times as pigheaded as a pighead," the next day, December 24 at 1:00 P.M., I renewed my request at the end of my interview with Henry Kissinger. Kissinger's reaction, so revealing in many ways, can be summed up in a few words:

K: How did you ask for the interview?

I: Through the regular channel, the State Department.

K: You made a mistake. You went to the wrong people. Why didn't you call me?

I: . . .?

He looked at his watch (it was 1:30 P.M.) and made a gesture for the telephone that connects him directly with the President. He checked himself and said that it was too late; the President would be having lunch. He then said that he would try to arrange a meeting for Saturday. In parting, he added that the request had not even been passed on by those people; proof of it was the fact that it did not go through his hands. . . .

9. He couldn't do anything for Saturday (Nixon went to Camp David for the weekend). Kissinger himself left for California to work on the new "State of the World" report that Nixon would present to Congress on February 15. But under the direction of General Haig, Kissinger's deputy, his office continued to work on the matter.

10. At last, on the morning of Wednesday the 30th, the day I was leaving Washington, General Haig himself called to tell me that the President would see me at noon.

11. General Haig was waiting for me and led me to the President's waiting room, where we sat for an hour. (There were many explanations for this unusual delay, due to an emergency meeting of the President with all the Senate leaders, but it was also a good opportunity to say a lot of things to the number-two man in Kissinger's office.)

12. I was shown in at 1:00 P.M. General Haig was also present. Nixon gave me a very hearty welcome, rising from his desk and coming to the door of the Oval Office to receive me and give

a thousand excuses for having made me wait an hour. He showed
that he was well up on the Chilean situation. He was enthusiastic
about many things; he recalled his visit to Chile, in 1966 I believe,
and he turned what could have been a short protocol visit of five
minutes into a pleasant, relaxed, and fast-moving thirty-minute
conversation. Twice, when I started to leave, he stopped me to
open a new theme or ask a question or add a remark.

13. He was very frank, stating his point of view about the political situation in Chile and the relations between the two countries. I shall repeat some of his phrases here:

"We are pragmatic. We're prepared to get along with anyone,
that's what we do.

"I can't hide the fact that the takeover by Chile's new government has worried us very much. But that shouldn't surprise you,
since that government apparently favors foreign policies that
contradict certain aspects of U.S. foreign policy. What Chileans
do in their domestic policy is obviously something that concerns
only them, and we have no part in it. But when it passes on to
foreign policy, and positions are taken that stand in the way of
our own foreign policy, we can't just sit back. On the contrary,
we would have to react according to the circumstances.

"It's quite clear that each country has a right to carry out a
policy of expropriations. We don't believe in it, but if a country
believes it is serving the interests of its people that way, it is free
to do it. However, if in the process the interests of American citizens and corporations are involved, and if they do not receive
adequate compensation, we would have to come out and defend
them, as any government would. There would be reprisals on our
part, *not* of a military type but of an economic nature.

"Unfortunately, I don't know President Allende. I hope he
has the vision and the power to preserve Chile's greatest values,
the things that give it prestige in the international community and
especially in this hemisphere: its history and its democratic tradition, its institutional stability, its pluralistic society. I've been
told that President Allende is a man of long-standing democratic
convictions. I repeat, I don't know him, so I can't judge for myself. But I do know that many of his followers are not like that.
That's why, I repeat, it depends on the President — and on the
opposition too — to preserve these values, this pluralistic society,
in Chile. That is what I, as a sincere friend of that country, hope
and desire.

"We are pragmatic. We get along and are ready to get along
with any country, with any kind of government. I think we have
proved this. Without going far for examples, there is that of
President Velasco in Peru. We don't want to confront anybody,

and we will not take such initiatives. But if we are given provocation, we'll know how to respond."[4]

14. One last observation: this interview granted by Nixon to
an ambassador leaving Washington is unusual, and, consequently
its political content is evident. The best proof of this — to one
who knows the psychology of the Nixon administration — is the
statement in the official communique of the White House, which
says that such an audience is not unusual. That is Nixon's "low
profile" . . . .

Domingo Santa María
December 31, 1970

The airs of a reasonable statesman assumed by Nixon after eight years
as vice-president, eight additional years of political discipline, and several years as president, did not completely hide, during this interview,
the threats of imperialism, *la bestia senza pace* of Dante's *Inferno*.
"When . . . positions are taken that stand in the way of our own foreign
policy, we can't just sit back." "We would have to react according to
the circumstances." "We would have to come out and defend [the
interests of American citizens and corporations]." "There would be
reprisals on our part . . . ." "If we are given provocation, we'll know
how to respond."

The very existence of the Allende government was a provocation to
the United States. In spite of moderate circumlocutions, Nixon could
not help saying at the beginning of the interview, "I can't hide the fact
that the takeover by Chile's new government has worried us very much."
Of course, he did not speak about the direct acts of aggression his
government had used against Chile in September and October (and
which were publicly revealed in March 1972 and March 1973) and the
policy decisions he had made in November 1970, already being applied
while he spoke to the Chilean ambassador.

Nor did he try to hide his arrogance. "I've been told that President
Allende is a man of long-standing democratic convictions. I repeat, I
don't know him, so I can't judge for myself. But I do know that many
of his followers are not like that. That's why, I repeat, it depends on the
President . . . ."

On the other hand, he puts on a show of cold indifference toward
Chile's domestic policy, saying, "What Chileans do in their domestic
policy is obviously something that concerns only them, and we have no
part in it" — distinguishing it, in a purely theoretical way, from the
foreign policy that concerns the United States. But under this deceitful

dialectic, he could not conceal the link between the internal situation of foreign countries and American foreign policy, between the public and private sectors of the United States; that is, the interests of American corporations.

8

The first principle of U. S. international policy is to give full protection to private interests. American private interests are the public interests of the U. S. government, the state policy of the empire.

Chile heard this axiom for the first time, wrapped up in the wise words of the statesman, at the meeting between its ambassador and President Nixon on December 30, 1970. The representatives of the Popular Unity government would hear it repeated many times, in increasingly cruder form, by the agents of the empire — notably at the rounds of bilateral talks on pending litigations (the last occurred in Washington in March 1973) and in Paris during the negotiations on Chile's foreign debt.

According to that first principle of U. S. international policy, nationalizations should be adequately compensated.

At this time, the nationalization of the great copper mining industry was being debated in the Chilean Congress. All the political parties in Chile, including those of the right wing (with Senator Francisco Bulnes as their spokesman), had expressed, at various times and in different forms, the urgent need for a total nationalization of the American companies exploiting Chile's copper. Proof that this was an absolute historical claim lies in the fact that a few months later, in the middle of 1971, the text of the constitutional reform bill authorizing this nationalization was unanimously ratified by Congress — after an exhaustive and impeccable parliamentary debate — with all parties participating. (This was regarded by everyone, including the People's Republic of China, as an extraordinary event.)

97

Allende's government applied this constitutional text so scrupulously that no one, in or outside of Chile, ever insinuated that Allende was violating it when the "excess profits" already taken by Kennecott and Anaconda were deducted from the indemnification, as the reform bill authorizing the nationalization stipulated. The Comptroller General of the Republic — whose office, together with the Supreme Court, was the domestic organization most hostile to the government[1] — calculated according to the law the deductions for excessive profits. The court that examined the demands for indemnification by the nationalized companies was accepted by those companies as legally valid during the long trial, in which Anaconda and Kennecott took part, down to the final ruling.

But, driven by its own state policy, the U. S. government started to pressure the Chilean government long before the reform bill was passed and became law. The Allende administration was ready for the legal, political, and economic arguments the Nixon administration and the corporations would develop while the nationalization law was being debated and after it went into effect. For years Chile had been preparing for the series of aggressive acts the American system would launch, with copper as a pretext.

A memorandum written before the plan for constitutional reform was sent to the Chilean Congress, on November 13, 1970, said, among other things:

> In cases of nationalization, "equitableness" (and the concept of equity) depends more on "the interests of the community" than it does in cases of expropriation.
>
> From a strictly constitutional point of view, nationalizations may lead to expropriations, but from the international juridical point of view, nationalizations (especially when basic resources are involved) have inherent traits that the courts must take into account (this has been done in other countries) when they interpret the constitutional settlement on expropriations resulting from nationalizations of this kind. Moreover, we must consider the U. N.'s resolution on the restitution of natural resources.
>
> As for the amount of indemnification, in all cases of nationalization since the last war, the calculation of it — as well as the interpretation of "equitableness" derived from it — was not carried out, juridically speaking, on a commutative basis but on a distributive basis. That is the only way equitableness takes in the basic concept of "the interests of the community." There are many precedents in history, as well as juridical, philosophical,

and moral arguments, not to mention economic considerations, to support this general assertion.

On December 21, when President Allende publicly signed the nationalization plan, another Chilean memorandum was written, analyzing the "legal arsenal" created by the United States, within its internal juridical system, to protect private investments abroad. Several of these laws, like the Hickenlooper and Sabbatino amendments, were enacted with special attention to anticipated nationalizations in Latin America, or in reaction to those carried out in Cuba. In the case of Chile, the U. S. system of insurance for private American interests abroad seemed best; AID[2] was in charge of this at first, and later on a mixed corporation called OPIC[3] took over. Since the insurance policies were paid by the American Treasury, they led to legal and political confrontations between governments on the subject of interests whose origin and nature were private. Finally, the Eximbank statutes also contain particular stipulations intended to dissuade Third World countries from showing any economic independence.

Memorandum

International aspects related to the constitutional settlement nationalizing copper

Although the "sanctioning" aspect of the Hickenlooper Amendment — calling for the suspension of economic aid to those countries whose nationalization methods were anticipated by this American law — is irrelevant in Chile's case (because it no longer receives such aid) the amendment is important because it establishes the "criterion" by which the United States judges the international legality or illegality of acts of nationalization. The United States would rely on this criterion in order to confront those countries in other areas and on other matters. It is worthwhile to remember that one part of the Hickenlooper Amendment refers to countries that have nationalized, expropriated, acquired, or taken over the control of property owned by an American citizen or corporation, company or association, where at least 50 percent of the property is in the hands of American citizens, and that another part of the same amendment extends to those cases where a country has taken measures to suspend or annul contracts or existing agreements with a U. S. citizen or corporation, company or association, in which no less than 50 percent is in American hands.

We should also keep in mind the Sabbatino Amendment (also embodied in article 620 of the U. S. law on foreign aid). Its object is to counterbalance the doctrine established by the U. S. Supreme Court in the "Sabbatino case" (derived from one of the Cuban nationalizations). In this doctrine, the Supreme Court decreed that the U. S. courts cannot rule on the validity of expropriations made by a sovereign foreign state recognized by the United States, in the case of private property situated within that country, when there exists no treaty or other agreement between the governments of the United States and the country in question to establish legal principles of control (of these situations) — even if the charges argue that these acts of expropriation or nationalization violate customary international rights. The Act of State doctrine, as it is called, established the international inviolability of the sovereign act of a foreign state and the lack of jurisdiction on the part of the United States not only to condemn it but also to judge it. Its validity was so foolproof that it was considered politically necessary to counterbalance it with an amendment or special law — which, of course, had no validity except in U. S. internal affairs. Thus the Sabbatino Amendment says:

"Notwithstanding any other provision of law, no court in the United States shall decline on the ground of the federal act of state doctrine to make a determination on the merits giving effect to the principles of international law in a case in which a claim of title or other right is asserted by any party including a foreign state (or a party claiming through such state) based upon (or traced through) a confiscation or other taking after January 1, 1959, by an act of that state in violation of the principles of international law, including the principles of compensation and the other standards set out in this subsection." This amendment carries two preliminary exceptions: 1) when an act of a foreign state is not contrary to international law; 2) "in any case with respect to which the President determines that application of the act of state doctrine is required in that particular case by the foreign policy interests of the United States . . . ."

The relevance of this settlement lies in the possibility that judicial proceedings will be opened at the initiative of American private interests in the U. S. courts, without the presence of representatives of the foreign state, leading to the expected public debate and eventually ending in embargo or some other judiciary measure.

On the other hand, the insurance system managed first by AID and now by OPIC, both agencies of the U.S. government (although OPIC tries to lighten the administrative burden of the federal government by handing part of the insurance over to private insurance companies — though not the responsibility to pay insurance in case of "accident" nor the legal consequences) refers equally to expropriation risks and other similar risks involving private American investments and properties in foreign countries. In accordance with the law that created it, this system operates even if — as in Chile's case — there is no governmental agreement with the United States concerning these risks or the corresponding insurance. In fact, this system operates as if the U. S. government agency were a private underwriter. But it has the following effects: (1) Once the American customer has exhausted the normal procedure for pressing claims against the act of nationalization (or expropriation, depending on the term preferred by American law), he puts himself under the category of risk insured by OPIC (or "victim of the accident"), and he demands the insurance payment from the U. S. government agency. This agency then examines the customer's claim and, at the same time, examines the development of the legal rights (and, of course, the act of nationalization), as well as the eventual judgment passed by the courts of the country in which the nationalization takes place on the private interests with regard to their compensation; for, considering the AID-OPIC insurance system, which was created precisely to bring about this situation, the American government can find itself having to pay the insurance once the foreign nationalization has taken place. This explains, from the American standpoint, why the U. S. government has "legitimate" worries, in the case of these nationalizations, about their consequences. (2) Once the customer has received the insurance money from OPIC, this agency legally takes the place (in terms of U. S. law) of the individual who was paid the insurance, assuming his rights and expectations; that is, it becomes the beneficiary of those rights and expectations, and as such it directly confronts the foreign government that nationalized. Of course, the latter can rightfully maintain that the act of nationalization only concerns the state that carried it out and the individuals affected, and not the government of the country with which these individuals have drawn up an insurance contract. But the mechanism of this insurance system gives, as its object, justification for U. S. government participation when it confronts the foreign government and tries to find the means to recover the insurance money.

Finally, we must keep in mind the statutory situation of Eximbank, which is really a U. S. government agency, whose statutes are founded on American law; they contain clauses that conform to the spirit and letter of the system described above, permitting punishment and, in response to acts of nationalization — depending on the kind of credit contracts endorsed — even provide for

claiming, through direct legal maneuvers, the corresponding payments. We can therefore say that Eximbank takes an active
part in the network of direct activity against a foreign state, because it performs an Act of State, under the orders of the U. S.
government.

Santiago, December 31, 1970

This text was completed a few days later with a study, somewhat more
detailed, of indemnification in cases of nationalization:

. . . c. Indemnification

The United States maintains, as it invariably has, that if
nationalization is to have international validity, an "adequate,
prompt, and effective" indemnification must be paid.

Here we must make a distinction between two different aspects:

One is the existence of the obligation to indemnify, and the
other is the establishment of the amount of compensation. The
first of these does not raise any problem, since the reform clearly
defines the responsibility to indemnify. Concerning the second,
the United States maintains that an "adequate" indemnification
is one that has a commutative character, representing the value
estimated by the expropriated; or that, to be equitable, it must be
very close to that estimate. From a strictly legal point of view,
we can argue about whether there exists in international law some
rule that directly refers to the amount of indemnification in such
terms that an amount less than what may be called the legal mean
value would make nationalization illegal. We can answer this
query by examining the usual practice among countries, especially since 1945; such an examination clearly indicates that practically no nationalization has resulted in a commutative indemnification, not even in the cases involving the United Kingdom and
France in 1946. Moreover, the nationalizations in Eastern Europe,
Indonesia, Ceylon, Tunisia, and Mexico, among others, led to
global agreements on indemnification, in which the amount
finally accepted by the country of the investors affected was
much lower than the commutative value. We submit Armando
Uribe's memorandum of January 5, "Precedents of indemnification amounts actually paid in cases of nationalizations abroad."

The basic reasons for maintaining that there are no principles
of international law regulating expropriation and linking it to
the payment of an "adequate, prompt, and effective" indemnification are as follows:

1. There is no international treaty ratifying it

2. Specific treaties in the past that may have been applicable have no general value, especially since the nationalizations that followed World War II

3. This idea is contradicted by the practice of nations after the war (and even before it, as we have already seen)

4. United Nations resolution 1803, almost unanimously approved with all the capitalist countries supporting the vote, gives the theory of nationalization its blessing, and speaks of "proportioned" indemnification, which is very different from "equitable" indemnification

5. Bilateral "lump-sum agreements" confirm the principles of nationalization and exclude those of classic expropriation

6. Expropriation in the classic sense (affecting foreign interests) is almost never carried out by governments

7. Expropriation with commutative indemnification is illogical, for it makes the act of nationalization rely for its validity not on legal bases but on how much the country in question can pay

On January 1, 1971, when the constitutional process of passing the reform amendment had just got under way, another memorandum added the following:

Ref. Preventive measures in case of eventual American reactions to the nationalization of copper

It should be noted that the special nature (perhaps without international precedent) of the nationalization of copper in Chile, which is being carried out by a constitutional amendment now going through the legislative stages, should hamper and slow down the eventual American reaction; even if the Chilean Government's intentions are made clear by the presentation of the plan itself, nationalization is not being put into effect before the bill is approved, and the United States cannot react at this time.

Yet, to evaluate the kind of eventual American reactions that may occur, we should remember the reference, already made by that government, to economic sanctions or reprisals if the interests of American citizens or corporations were affected — that is, if they did not receive adequate compensation; these are reactions that are already having a political impact, although it is before the fact, from a legal point of view.

Not long after this, a collective study, headed by Foreign Minister

Clodomiro Almeyda, completed these analyses, observing at the same time:

> The effects of nationalization on various aspects of the international relations between Chile and the government of the United States have obviously not been considered in the present study; for example, its effects on the importation of equipment, technology, and spare parts from the United States, on which we are strongly dependent; or its indirect effects on the financial systems of Europe, Japan, and other countries that export capital; or, in general, the notable influence the U. S. government can exert on the multinational sources of international finance, like the World Bank (and its affiliates) and the Inter-American Development Bank — sources that have been very important to the public sector of Chile for the past few years.
>
> Nor have we considered the future effects any action of the American government could have on the international commerce in Chilean products, not only through bilateral measures, but also through measures that could distort Chile's trade with other countries as well as the world market for Chilean products.

The most thorough report on foreign policy for this period is dated January 28, 1971. It examined some of the possible U. S. reprisals against Chile, prompted by political motives, and mentioned the following:

> 1. A decision by Eximbank to cut off those lines of credit in financial operations with Chile which would set an example and would probably heavily influence private banks and other financial centers in the United States and in Third World countries
>
> 2. A decision by American enterprises to take their claims before the courts of all the countries that import copper from Chile's great mining industries, accompanied by petitions demanding embargo and other preventive measures, and maintaining that nationalizations are internationally illegal, by these terms, with special reference to indemnification; also, that the act of nationalization cannot transfer the copper to the Chilean state, and that control of it, or at least the responsibility for the commercial operations of its sale, should revert to the firms in question.

In the face of these and other possible measures, some Chilean countermeasures were studied. For example, with regard to an eventual embargo in Europe and other countries, the following was considered:

In the event that actions to regain possession are brought by the companies before the courts of countries that import Chilean copper, Chile can count on many legal defenses; thus, the American enterprises (Anaconda, Kennecott, etc.) cannot press claims nor ask for preventive measures concerning Chilean copper, because they do not actually have (nor have they had during the past few years) direct ownership of the copper, not only as a result of nationalization — the validity of which cannot be contested internationally — but also because the copper has been under the control of joint stock companies established in Chile in which the American enterprises hold minority stock.

This defense was not premature; the United States was already launching its attack.

On March 29, while Congress was studying the plan for nationalization, Ambassador Korry, then still at his post, had an interview with Foreign Minister Clodomiro Almeyda. The following memo was drawn up from that meeting:

He told him that the arrangement of the plan, in its present stage, would imply the "annulment" of commitments made by the previous government, especially with respect to the operative methods for effecting the prompt payment for the stock (51 percent) bought by Chile; and, specifically, everything that had to do with promissory notes on New York banks.

Regarding indemnification, he insisted that it must be based on the commercial value — including the value of the mineral deposits not yet exploited — and that it must be prompt and effective besides. Referring in particular to the deductions from the indemnification, considered in the plan as justified by the "excess profits" made by the companies, he said that they were (1) a form of punishment against the companies; (2) a hostile gesture toward the United States; and (3) very unjust because the U. S. government had guaranteed the investments of those companies on the basis of commitments made by previous administrations.

From these observations, we can assume that to the U. S. government the norms of the plan in matters of indemnification, and specifically those which refer to deductions for excessive profits, have the following characteristics: (1) they are not valid internationally; (2) they represent reprisals against the companies and economic aggression toward the United States.

We can also indirectly deduce that the U. S. government objects to the standards for indemnification, particularly those refer-

ring to "excess profits," as long as there is a chance that it might
become the eventual beneficiary of indemnification in accordance
with its insurance system.

It also follows that, for the American government, the indemnification for the value of unexploited mining deposits must form
a part of the indemnified commercial value.

Taking all this into account, as well as the whole nationalization
procedure, the ambassador insisted that the Chilean government
should take a more flexible position. By this, as we can see from
various parts of his statement, he meant that the government
should (a) modify those aspects of the plan that he had pointed
out, and (b) negotiate with the companies themselves on all these
points, before the plan is approved. He offered the assistance
of his government in getting the negotiations under way.
He indicated that if what was just described in (a) and (b)
above is not pursued, all of these questions will degenerate into
litigation proceedings at intergovernmental level, and that this
will impair relations between the United States and Chile.

These official statements of Korry's, anticipated long before in the studies
made by the Chilean government, meant that the United States had
opened fire. Not only was it banging menacingly on the table but, moreover, these threats were being made on behalf of strictly private American concerns, suggesting that the government was willing to help out in
the matter. The official myth of American noninterference in private
affairs, which Robert Kennedy had mentioned in Chile five years before,
was once more being disproved: ". . . if what was just described . . .
is not pursued, all of these questions will degenerate into litigation proceedings at intergovernmental level, and this will impair relations between
the United States and Chile." The interests of the private companies
were the interests of the United States. If Chile did not yield, the U. S.
government was ready to step in; and to prove this, it threatened to use
all its sanctioning power ("this will impair relations . . .") unless Chile
accepted some other kind of intervention first (which Korry called
"the assistance of his government in getting negotiations under way.")
And with these declarations, Korry obviously meddled in Chilean
affairs; he made serious threats to the Chilean government while the
plan for constitutional reform was following its normal course in
Congress.

But the American position showed another important characteristic:
in early 1971, before nationalization went into effect, and even before
it was approved, the United States had already chosen the official ter-

rain on which it would bring out into the open its conflict with Chile — the nationalization of copper.

For the United States, this would be — as Charles Meyer was to say more than once in Washington — the "rock in the road" of relations between the two countries. In official American declarations this would be, during the coming years, the pending question and the unresolved conflict between them. Ah, if one could only move "the rock," there would be no problems between the United States and Chile . . . .

The American government kept this question pending all those years. It brought it up again and again at every meeting. It even refused to allow the application of the solemn Treaty for the Solution of any Difficulties that might arise between Chile and the United States of America, which was signed in Washington in 1914, ratified by both countries, and still valid in 1973 — a basic document for the relations between the two nations.

The Nixon administration had to keep the question of copper open. This was its only cover-up for the much graver acts of aggression it was committing and escalating against Chile.

And yet, it was a very flimsy cover-up. The nature of the nationalization of Chilean copper; the impeccable juridical and political way in which the national measure was adopted (a scrupulous reform of the Constitution of the State approved unanimously by Congress); the debate before the courts, with the companies present, and the adverse decision on the establishment of indemnifications; the deduction, set by the comptroller general, for excess profits; the really excessive benefits the companies had received from their Chilean operations (enormously damaging to Chile, and several times more than Anaconda and Kennecott received during the same years from their mines in the United States and in other countries); the juridical formula for the "deduction of excessive profits," difficult to attack internationally in theory and practice, before foreign courts, and even more so in the United Nations and other political forums — all this prevented the United States from exploiting far and wide the issue on which it had chosen to carry out officially its international controversy with Chile.

The U. S. government had never had to face such problems in other cases of nationalization of their investments. The Chilean affair could not be considered as "plunder" or a "takeover" that was either arbitrary, discriminating, a denial of justice, or alien to accepted international law.

Politically speaking, no one could argue that here was an illegitimate government acting by force. The government of Chile was legitimate, Chile was a democracy, with separation of powers; the rule of law prevailed; it recognized the moral and physical liberties of the people and respected civil rights more than in other democracies; foreigners and nationals were equal before the law, and the rights of companies, like everyone's, were guaranteed in accordance with internal laws and international rights. Chile was in the right. Nationalization was unassailable. The United States never dared take the matter to the International Court of Justice in The Hague. Most of the measures studied by the Chilean government to counter any eventual legal attacks by the Americans never had to be used. In 1972 when Kennecott initiated embargo proceedings against Chilean copper in European countries, it wanted to upset the market for it, making it seem as if Chilean copper were in litigation. The proceedings failed; U. S. tactics were to keep the legal proceedings pending as long as possible to distort the Chilean copper market, but those they tried to keep going were not being decided in Kennecott's favor, and several of the firm's claims had already been turned down.

All of this was accompanied by political action: the U. S. ambassadors visited the ministers of foreign relations in the European capitals where the trials took place, to explain the U. S. government's interest in the matter. However, the European countries already understood that these embargo proceedings against copper represented the Nixon administration's political desire to crush Chile in any way possible. The nationalization of copper was used as an explicit symbol of its essential conflict with Chile and of its unyielding attitude toward the Popular Unity government.

It was not the best instrument, but it was the only one they could use in public. Furthermore, the Chilean formula for indemnification and the doctrine of excess profits (called the Allende doctrine) signalled new risks for investors at a time when nationalizations were multiplying, precisely because they were so legally sound and their international presentation so foolproof.

In short, the nationalization of copper was the only international justification the Nixon administration could find to use for its action against Chile. This, in itself, was not a good pretext, and did not provide sufficient motive for aggression. As there were no other formal grounds for a dispute available, the United States publicly made copper the center of its conflict with Chile.

But this choice was purely tactical. In this conflict, copper was just a pretext. The real object of the conflict was Chile itself.

The United States tried to create an impression of prudence and moderation in the eyes of the world in its initial application of the policy decided upon in November 1970. A democracy like Chile — with a legitimate government capable of withstanding intrigues of the kind used against it in September and October and which had captured the attention of numerous countries — could not be treated publicly as a nation and government that was breaking international law.

Dr. Kissinger once called together a group of newsmen for a background briefing, to speak of his government's attitude toward Chile. This method, which he used so frequently between 1969 and 1973, to get across to the public, through the news media, ideas that were of tactical advantage to the United States at the moment (remember how useful this was for U. S. policy in Vietnam and Indochina[1]) fascinated the newsmen and made them docile vehicles for the ideas Dr. Kissinger wanted to disseminate. These briefings, and many others like them, were a kind of policy at a distance, a "message" used to hide the real policy, rather than an honest declaration of intentions and points of view. On the other hand, at this early stage, it was not only possible but useful for the United States to reassure Chile and the rest of the world about its good intentions; from November on, its policy was to let the Chilean experiment continue, so that the country could gradually deteriorate, with the help of economic and other aggressions, and so serve as an example and a warning to Third World countries.

An Associated Press dispatch dated January 3, 1971, from Washington (which was published in *El Mercurio*) had this to say:

> Two months after the takeover by a leftist government in Chile, the United States seemed determined to avoid any measure which might push that country into the Soviet bloc.
>
> U. S. policy was described last week by a high-ranking White House official who declared that an attitude of overt hostility on the part of the United States toward the government of Salvador Allende might engender an outburst of nationalist sentiment in Chile which could result in forcing that country to abandon the 'American community.' "If Chile turns toward Cuba," said this high official, "it would be difficult to pretend that the United States had not pushed it there . . . . Channels of communication with Chile will remain open."
>
> This high official, who cannot be identified, is the same official who gave some very alarmist opinions on Chilean events during an interview with some journalists shortly after the Chilean elections of September 4.
>
> At that time, he predicted that the Allende government would create "massive problems" for the United States and he could sense disturbance on the side of the Inter-American Council of Defense and the OAS.
>
> In the course of last week's press conference, this same official did not reiterate his former preoccupations; instead he gave the impression that the United States has been, in fact, somewhat relieved by the attitude and activities of the Chilean government during the last several months. Allende had reestablished diplomatic relations with Cuba and had announced plans for the nationalization of American mining interests in Chile, but none of these actions appeared to greatly concern White House officials. They observed that the new government had failed to directly criticize the United States and had promised to indemnify the American mining companies. Other reasons led these officials to think that Chile would not become a "second Cuba." They are noting that Castro, in comparison to Allende, had not been elected Chief of State and that he did not have a congress to which he had to account for his actions.
>
> Besides, Allende's promised revolution does not show so clearly the anti-American traits and feelings that Castro's revolution has shown in the last decade. The United States seems determined this time to avoid any action against Chile which could be considered provocative . . . .

It was symptomatic. This "high-ranking White House official," "the same official who gave some very alarmist opinions on Chilean events during an interview with some journalists shortly after the Chilean elections" (that is, in his briefing in Chicago on September 16, from which the January dispatch quotes literally), now refrained from repeating his "former preoccupations." In fact, when he referred to "the nationalization of American mining interests in Chile," which, he said, was one of the plans announced by Allende (the Chilean government had already made public the complete text of the constitutional amendment on nationalization), Kissinger declared before his audience that none of those actions disturbed White House officials very much. But right after that, he emphasized, with typical diplomatic cunning, that Chile "had promised to indemnify the American mining companies." Chile had promised nothing, either way. The government of Chile simply had sent the national Congress a constitutional amendment that considered, at one and the same time, indemnification and the legal deductions called for.

Kissinger's moderate phrasing gives an idea of the style of apparent rectitude the United States would publicly adopt, until March 1973, every time it referred to Chile. It was trying to lull public opinion and, if possible, the Chilean government itself. This time the United States seemed determined to avoid "any action against Chile that could be considered provocative," precisely in order to carry out more effectively its clandestine activities in the economic field and to pave the way for future intervention. In reality, this deceptive language, which made it easy for Americans, even after the coup, to show dismay and even indignation, if not downright self-righteousness, when accused of aggression, was an integral part of the system of political intervention they had decided to apply in Chile. The apparent decision ("the United States *seems* determined this time to avoid any action against Chile which could be *considered* provocative") expressed the method they had chosen to cover their provocations. That Chile was an invisible and silent Vietnam was not just a random postulation. The official American attitude toward Chile described by Kissinger in January 1971 corresponded line by line to what it already had been, according to State Department authorities, in the second half of 1970. (All we have to do is to recall the words of the high official to the Chilean journalist J. M. Navasal, and the observation contained in the Chilean study of August 1970 about the position of the State Department, which reflected many conversations with Charles Meyer and other authorities in the State

Department.) This confirms the fact that in November Kissinger and the White House had chosen the plan worked out by the State Department and made it part of the National Security Council's general scheme. Under cover of lulling words about nonintervention, in September and October the provocative measures (of which we already know) were carried out, on orders from the highest level of government. And behind Kissinger's deceptive new talk of noninterference, well-known acts of provocation would be perpetrated.

How many other points of view about Chile must have been expressed by Henry Kissinger between 1971 and 1973? We do not have written records of these available right now. However, we do have something even more revealing — accounts of specific acts of aggression.

Considering the financial aspect alone, for a few tangible examples of United States' general action against Chile all we have to do is go to Chapter II of an unpublished study by two high-ranking Chilean officials who noted in 1973:

> An important part of the strategy to block and destroy the people's government has been played on this terrain. Financial strangulation is the least visible way to attack the country; this was behind the actions of private American banks, government financing agencies like Eximbank and AID, and international organizations on which the United States exerts a decisive influence. Thus, the rapid flight of capital which took place right after the elections was followed by a quick restriction of credits granted by organizations which have traditionally carried on these financial operations with Chile.[2] All we have to do is to set down some facts:
>
> *a.* In July 1971, Eximbank rejected a request for credit to buy airplanes.
>
> *b.* In that same period, the State Department sent letters to its representatives in IDB and the World Bank directing them to turn down requests for credit from countries which expropriate without compensation.
>
> *c.* From 1971 on, public statements by President Nixon, Secretary of State Rogers, and other officials implied that expropriations without compensation could affect foreign aid to underdeveloped countries, constituting a warning not only to Chile but also to the Third World, and putting pressure on other dependent countries to contribute to Chile's isolation.
>
> *d.* In addition to this, in January 1972 Braden Co. took direct action, and asked that Chilean copper be incorporated. It attached the accounts of the principal Chilean government agen-

cies in the United States. Later, this firm tried to enlist various
European countries to start embargoes against Chile.

e. In February 1972, Anaconda opened proceedings against
CODELCO and asked for an embargo on the CODELCO and
CORFO assets.[3] This stopped shipment of spare parts and other
goods of CODELCO's which were under the embargo.

f. American banks gradually reduced their financing of import
operations as follows:

Nov. 1970	$220 million
Nov. 1971	$88 million
Jan. 1972	$36 million
Dec. 1972	$32 million

g. Since the Popular Government came to power, Chile has not
received a single loan from the World Bank, although it has prepared and turned in proposals that fulfilled the current conditions
for loans. Since the strategic sectors and enterprises of the
economy depend upon the United States, the reduction and interruption of credits from private, government, and international
banks, as well as technological restrictions that would slow down
the shift of Chile's trade to other countries, show America's intention to interfere decisively in the functioning of Chile's economy.

Under the circumstances, the country had to use its resources
abroad to keep up the normal course of the economy, and it had
to restrict the payment of its foreign debt. In 1971 these payments reached 35 percent of the value of our exports. The government sought a way out of this problem by renegotiating the
national indebtedness.

In general, we can say that the strategy followed by the various
interested parties was the same, but their tactics differed.

Private American banks adopted a more flexible line than the
U. S. government for the renegotiation of the debt. They agreed
to refinance it over an eight-year period. These agreements were
reached before the renegotiation with the governments and their
agencies in the United States, Europe, and Japan, and their terms
were very favorable for Chile. (We must emphasize that the
transference of American banks to the public sector in Chile was
effected on the basis of direct negotiations that resulted in agreement between both parties.)

On the other hand, the financing institutions of the U. S. government — Eximbank and AID — adopted a tougher attitude. The
importance of the suppression of long-term credits by the U. S.
government is evident; in the past few years, almost 50 percent of
equipment was imported from the United States (this reached
90 percent and 100 percent in certain key enterprises), with the
principal industries importing an even higher percentage of Ameri-

can materials. As a result, the renovation of the industrial plants and, consequently, the maintenance of the levels of productive activity were seriously affected by this financial restriction.

The U. S. government's pressure on the World Bank and the Inter-American Development Bank resulted in the suspension of credits for investment in projects that already had been approved. As we have pointed out, this control over international organizations is explained by the interrelation between them and the large corporations and private financing institutions that provide the above-mentioned banks with equipment and capital.

There was also pressure from the American government on the European countries. In renegotiating its debt, Chile requested a settlement allowing it to postpone payment for four years, but managed to get a delay of only one year. The United States made indemnification of the copper companies a prerequisite for any multilateral negotiation and finally settled on a one-year agreement.

The strategy used by the American government to divert or stop the Chilean phenomenon was the result of a large number of factors involving the intervention of concerned private interests, but these factors were considered with an eye on the near or even distant future, looked at in an international context that was rapidly evolving. These factors led to the adoption of some of the measures atypical of American behavior in the past when faced with political processes that affect its interests.

The complexity of the domestic and international centers of power that determine American policy is such that we have to oversimplify the United States, to treat it as if it were a moral person with only one voice, represented by those who officially run it, and who are identifiable by their names and positions. But the U. S. government is the central headquarters of a system of power whose centripetal forces never stop working and, in the long run, its various interests are incorporated into the imperialist system of monopolistic international capitalism (a monster that corrupts even language!); they blend together to become a supreme stock market of values or powers, a clearinghouse for vital interests — the U. S. government. The more concentrated this power is as we go up the scale to the top of this government, the more clear-cut this rationalizing operation becomes — if you can find out anything about it, which does not happen very often. Latin America, and for that matter the whole world, would give anything to understand the pressures that a huge number of American interests — with multinational corporations in the lead — bring to bear on their government from within, in order to have their own policies implemented; they would give anything to get a good look at the decisions and actions of the American government and compare them to the international policies that those corporations set for themselves.

From the experience of Chile — which has the advantage of numerous documents recording the connection between all of this, and which has served as a "test case" for this phenomenon of interaction between ITT (one of the most dynamic and politically conscious of the multinational corporations) and the White House — we can reach certain preliminary conclusions that can be useful in other case studies:

1. Although the multinational corporation seems to be, or believes itself to be, developing and carrying out its own foreign policy in another country, it actually *represents* — both in the dramatic and in the legal meaning of the word — the entire system, and unintentionally acts in behalf of interests that are "superior" to its own, since it has projected the public image of a state with its own structure and has identified itself with the American "cause."

2. Even if it is not in touch or in league with the authorized diplomatic or secret agents of the United States (and it is, since they often work for it as supernumeraries or even as advisors) the multinational corporation releases a parallel international policy which both influences and is influenced by the "official" one, and which in times of crisis abroad, becomes one with that policy.

3. The foreign policy of the multinational corporation serves as an instrument to put into effect the government's decisions; however, it often acts at a pace that is neither possible nor practical for that government. Thus, a company usually rehearses or practices what the government will act out in the near future. This works to the advantage of both: by trying out a policy before the government does, the company urges or eventually forces the government to apply it, and allows the government to test the effectiveness of a policy with less risk than when it commits itself directly or ahead of time; on the other hand, if the company's attempt is not successful, the government can scrap that particular policy and try others that are not as risky or as difficult.

4. A fourth conclusion, related to the first, is that a single powerful multinational firm (the real test of its strength is its economic and political importance within the system as a whole, not just in the foreign country) can represent all American private interests acting in the foreign country, even those which appear to be more important there. It assumes the role of general delegate for all of them.

5. A last preliminary conclusion, linked to the third, is that the errors committed by a multinational enterprise, which may seem important and may be financially costly and may even turn into an open scandal, are not errors or faults of the System; on the contrary, they are used to correct any defects in the System and to make it operate more efficiently in this or any other similar case. As the official center of the System, the American government may even be able to use such an error to apply, through publicly revealing this error or condemning it, the very policy that led to the error; nobody loses anything this way, neither the corporation nor the government, nor, above all, the System. As a matter of fact, they both turn the error into an asset; in other words, there was no error, after all. What we have just said, of course, takes place when there is a high level of interest in an international incident of this kind and the participants are very important.

All the conclusions we have just set down — except the last, which the exposé of the ITT plot at the Senate hearings in March 1973 will illustrate — come from analyzing the ITT documents and the dealings and correspondence between ITT and the American government regarding Chile between September 1970 and September 1971 — sources which can be completely trusted.

Between August and September 1971, while ITT representatives were in Chile negotiating with the Allende government the terms of its purchase of their telephone network (meanwhile, the other investments they had there, including hotels, were thriving and would continue to prosper during the entire Popular Unity administration), their president, Harold Geneen, was having lunch at the White House with Nixon's assistant for international economic affairs, Peterson, and with General Haig, Kissinger's deputy. He told them he felt sure that the ITT subsidiary would be taken over in Chile and that he was worried about the situation in that country.

Weeks later, the Allende administration named an "intervenor" to manage the Compañia de Teléfonos de Chile (Telephone Company of Chile), an excellent administrative move authorized by the law and in keeping with the company's legal statute, and not (as Sampson says in his description of these incidents) "a discreet form of nationalization." In the past, public utilities like this one had often been subjected to this type of control. But this time ITT decided that its Vice-President Merriam should write to Peterson suggesting all-out intervention to overthrow Allende: "Everything should be done quietly but effectively to see that Allende does not get through the crucial next six months."

An eighteen-point plan was suggested. Among these points were the following: the White House should set up "a special task force" to pressure Chile; all credits from American or foreign banks should be cut off, with the White House supporting the move; they should stir up discontent among Chile's armed forces; they should subsidize *El Mercurio*, Agustín Edwards's newspaper; Chile's foreign policy should be crippled; the CIA should take part in the "six-month squeeze."

The points of the plan enclosed with Merriam's letter — a plan that, at the hearings in March 1973, Peterson said he had never read — are well known.[4] Even if they had not been made public, we should have learned about them, simply because they were actually carried out. (Sampson, whose book was published before the coup, wrote, "How far this ITT pressure, whether through Peterson or anyone else, took effect is still obscure. . . .")

The six crucial months that ITT suggested to the White House should have been extended, according to the latter, not out of consideration or generosity, but because of the overall interests and perspectives of the System; not because the Nixon administration was less zealous than ITT, but actually because it was more so.

There was a lot still to be done if Chile's experience was to be a lesson for the rest of the world, but it would take time.

Chile's foreign indebtedness had to be used. The Paris Club still had to meet.

In our description of the American financial attacks, the study just cited refers to the way the Allende government was forced to renegotiate the enormous foreign debt it had inherited. According to this study, the strategies used against Chile by the various agencies "coincided" though their tactics differed.

The Paris Club[5] was a perfect forum for the United States in its conflict with Chile. It brought up the copper question, using the solution of the indemnification problem as a condition for the renegotiation of the debt — a problem that the Nixon administration really did not want solved at that time, for reasons we have already seen; besides, it knew there could be no solution. At the same time, the United States created a skillful division of interests among the various creditors by allowing or even encouraging renegotiation for certain countries and banks and by blocking others. Chile's foreign debt per capita was so large (they said that only Israel's surpassed it) that, obviously, when Popular Unity assumed power, all of the creditors should have wanted the Chilean experiment to be successful and should have guaranteed the necessary viability for its economic development. This was reinforced by the fact that future annual payments, according to the terms of the contracts, probably would be even larger than the corresponding needs of the annual flow of hard money (foreign exchange) coming in. Therefore, with its own interests in mind, the financial community was inclined to ignore political prejudices and grant easy terms to Chile.

The United States took advantage of this favorable attitude and let it run its course, but at the same time it politicized the question — giving indemnification priority, making other demands, setting up the one-year payment plan, etc. But above all, they made the most of the fact that, after the first round of Paris Club meetings, some creditors had renegotiated while others had not, and that financially speaking, the creditors were no longer unanimously in favor of helping the Salvador Allende administration. From then on, the United States could step up its plans of aggression against Chile without contradicting, at any moment, the impressive number of creditors whose main interest, *before this maneuver*, had been Chile's solvency and, therefore, its stability, since they did not feel their own credits threatened. Besides, at the Paris Club the United States obtained a yearly payment plan for Chile, since the negotiation of the debt had to be renewed the following year, with all the internal and international political consequences this would imply; it even obtained a psychological advantage over the Popular Unity administration and over the attitude of Third World countries toward it, thus keeping its privileged vantage point for American extortion in Chile.

While the Chileans were studying preventive measures to confront possible American reprisals for the nationalization of copper in early 1971, they felt that actions like the European embargo on copper would not take place until after an eventual renegotiation of the Chilean foreign debt. This was exactly what happened when Kennecott pressed charges.

After this Paris Club round, the U. S. economic squeeze became much more open. In the meantime, Chile followed the stipulations of its constitutional reform and continued to pay all its debts to the copper companies — hundreds of millions of dollars . . . .

October 1972 arrived. Everyone believed that, with all these blows, conditions were now ripe for the government's overthrow; and the second big reactionary upheaval took place.

Four senators, speaking for the opposition in planned but slightly varied speeches, declared that the government was becoming increasingly illegitimate. They spoke of the "illegitimate exercise" of power, inventing an expression unheard of in Chile. Another senator, a lawyer and Christian of the Left, said that they were looking in St. Thomas Aquinas for a legitimate excuse to start an armed uprising.

To anyone knowing the Chilean ruling class's love for legalistic things — since the juridical structure protects the status quo — it was evident that there would be a serious crisis.

It erupted a few days later. Truck owners in the far southern province of Aysen — which had a small population, was poorly developed, and had no railroads — went on strike, on the pretext that the government was trying to nationalize transportation in their province. The government explained that for a long time it had had the idea of starting a state transportation company for Aysen, which would still leave plenty of room for the private truck owners. They, however, took their case to the National Association of Truck Owners, and a nationwide strike was called. Other private federations joined them: small and medium-size enterprises, professional groups, and others. For two years, wholesalers — relying for support on their organization, the Chilean Association of Manufacturers and Merchants — had been intensifying their active campaign to recruit and mobilize as many people as they could in the whole country, naming people right and left proprietor, manufacturer, or merchant. A more important factor was the traditional dependence of the small manufacturer and merchant on supplies and economic credit mechanisms distributed by the Sociedad de Fomento Fabril and others coordinated by the Association. In the professional unions, well divided politically, left-wing doctors, lawyers, engineers, and the like were a minority. Even the administrations of the universities were generally controlled by the opposition.

But the strike, which was heavily financed by clandestine dollars, fell through. The Chilean people rallied as they never had before. Industry and agriculture went on producing, preventing a stoppage loss, under the management of workers and against the wishes of the owners. It was an experience of popular control of economic power. The antigovernment subversion resulted in more risk for the owners than for the government. The reactionaries laid down their arms. There were complex political negotiations, with a commander in chief of the Army, General Prats, present in the cabinet for the first time, and the strike was officially dead.

Sedition was the method used by the opposition; it was also the method of imperialism.

From the end of 1970 on, its main policy would be to instigate situations like that of October 1972, which would bring on the economic crash — with all its social and political consequences — which the United States had been ripening with such dedicated care.

The economic situation had reached a critical point, and the problems seemed ripe, but instead of falling, Allende came out of the crisis a stronger man.

He could go on a successful international tour and denounce, before the United Nations, the aggressions Chile had to bear and the stratagems of the multinational American corporations, which threatened the sovereignty of many countries.

How did the United States face this emergency? It followed three courses of action.

First, it intensified its economic squeeze of Chile abroad. It was not just a coincidence that Kennecott brought charges in France, demanding the embargo of important shipments of copper (with immediate effects on the market) on October 4, while the President's "illegitimate" actions were being debated in Santiago. Diplomats and other American representatives discreetly began to let it be known in the Third World that the U. S. government was in favor of these embargoes and similar actions, and how strongly it felt about Chile.

Secondly, the United States strengthened its contacts with certain elements of the Chilean armed forces and gave them increased opportunities to buy armaments, vehicles, and so forth, in the United States. It also consolidated its ties with certain members of the Chilean right wing, and in October it financed, secretly but directly, the massive mobilization of the truck owners and shopkeepers. Secret intelligence agents spread their nets even wider.

And finally, after the October strike was frustrated by the people, the United States proposed direct bilateral talks on pending problems. It was a dramatic stroke, a bolt out of the blue. Did Washington, then, believe that a dialogue between the United States and Chile was still possible?

A dialogue, a first round of bilateral talks, seemed possible to Washington because it would be nothing but words. In Chile, this partly encouraged the idea that its conflicts with the United States could still be resolved; it permitted the United States firsthand knowledge of the mood of the Chileans and their feelings toward the United States; it kept "pending questions" in limbo; and lastly, it lulled Chile's attention and even its ability to counterattack against those American measures already discussed, in and outside the country.

Bilateral conversations took place, with analyses made before and after them. Of course they came to nothing; they merely set the next round of talks for March, in Washington.

Referring to events in October 1972, one could think, once again, that everything in this book about events in Chile points to all of the plans and actions of American imperialism and ignores the importance of the actions and inactions of the Chilean reactionaries in the crisis, and even the role of the Allende government and the working class on which it was based.

The important role played by domestic forces is not forgotten. But what we are recording here is the continued interference in Chilean events of a great power that has largely determined these events, because it is much stronger than anyone or anything in Chile; a power which, when it did not directly provoke crises, stimulated them through "Pavlovian" measures designed to produce conditioned responses in economic and sociological areas, or which took advantage of those crises when they arose, hastening the process of disintegration. We are here recording American aggressions and intervention in Chile — not the role of Chile's reactionaries or even the role of its government, except when it is indispensable for the study of specific imperialist actions.

Thus, the author of this history should not be condemned for recording only what he has written here.

The American course of action, in response to the October crisis, was intended to rally the opposition and prepare more serious crises. But the intensification and obviousness of the economic blockade were designed to so aggravate the internal economic difficulties — by inflation, food shortages, difficulties of distribution, production slowdowns, and, if possible, unemployment — that, for specific economic and psychological reasons, it was believed that a large part of the electorate would vote against the government in the general elections to renew all of Congress and half of the Senate on March 4, 1973. The right wing was sure that this would happen. As a result of the paralysis of certain sectors in the economy's organization (which, it had been proved, were at the mercy of a seditious minority), the economic effects of the October strike had been very costly — the equivalent of a huge natural disaster, like an earthquake — adding up to millions of dollars.

Inflation was serious, and the problems of distribution had not been solved in spite of attempts to create new solutions. One part of the right wing thought it would obtain the two thirds of the seats in Parliament necessary to oust Allende. The other part was not so sure, but they believed that Popular Unity's setback would be considerable and that Allende would either have to mend his ways completely or resign.

None of this occurred on March 4. In these first general elections since Allende had come to power (the municipal elections of March 1971, in which Popular Unity had come out on top with 50 percent of the votes, had less political significance), Popular Unity had strengthened its position with a gain of almost 10 percent over the presidential elections, which in Chile was something unprecedented for a government already halfway through its mandate. None of the predictions came true. The government's firm political base was being strengthened by the crises. Thus, it seemed likely that, by rectifying certain social and economic conditions, the popular Chilean movement would grow to the point where it could not be turned back.

Popular Unity prepared itself for this; the analysis of the elections by the different parties was supplemented in several cases by analyses of the social behavior within the structure of Chilean society at this time. Both kinds of analyses demonstrated that the March vote had been an unprecedented class vote; it would only be a question of time and of following the correct political line, before the largest social class, knowing where their interests lay, would become an immovable bloc, establishing its rightful position and its identity as a class.

In the meantime, the class struggle already was being pushed to its limits by the bourgeoisie and by the actions of imperialism — an alliance that, in practice, does not hesitate to make a social analysis, appreciating and making the most of the political possibilities of the class struggle for its own benefit.

The results in March indicated that this time the alliance was losing the struggle. This was the most pressing danger for those who followed events in Chile with apprehension. Now, they would have to double their efforts.

On March 27, the President had thanked Commander in Chief Prats for his collaboration and that of the other ministers who were members of the armed forces. Then he formed a civilian cabinet.

Allende was well aware that this was a transcendent moment for Chile, but he was not the kind of man to see the dark side of things and give up. He dined that night at the Commander in Chief's home and

talked in high spirits about the various combinations possible for forming a new cabinet completely made up of civilians. His speech that
morning had mentioned the role of the armed forces in Chile:

> I believe we must stress the fact that the government, especially
> after the participation of representatives of the armed forces in
> the Cabinet, has to trace a plan of activities for these forces and
> assure them a more active and dynamic part in the great national
> task we have been carrying out with such determination and will;
> at the same time, that great sense of professional responsibility
> which characterizes our military institutions must be preserved.
> I believe a country's development and its security go together.
> I believe that if national defense is the fundamental task of the
> armed forces, they must contribute their experience and technol-
> ogy to the work of economic development which goes hand in
> hand with national security.

This reference to the need for the national defense staff to become a
permanent work force reflected a profound and recent experience
which showed the lack of unity and coordination between the different
branches of the armed forces. It was around this time, at the Air Force's
anniversary ceremonies, that its commander in chief, General Ruiz
Danyau (who gave way to the junta's General Leigh a few days before
the coup, and became the first "armed rector" of the University of
Chile) declared in a solemn address before the President of the Republic,
the other commanders, civil, religious, and diplomatic authorities, and
the Aviation Academy, that it was the sacred mission of his forces to see
that all aircraft and air troops were concentrated in the Air Force alone,
and that they would never give up until they had accomplished this.
He also mentioned the tridimensional doctrine, which the nonprofes-
sionals present did not understand; it was a reference to the military
principle — which was rather confidential — of coordinating the plans of
the three branches of the armed forces in case of foreign war. The
President had to improvise a few words to break the ice formed by
these remarks, especially among the top leaders in the Navy, which had
increased its aviation forces in the past few years and was proud of it.
   On March 27, President Allende also described the political and
economic blockade formed against him by the reactionary opposition
within and outside the country:

. . . We have to break out of the vicious circle they have built around us by not letting us pass the financial laws we need to set the national budget or adjust it; by subjecting us to an international aggression destined to isolate Chile, cutting down its credits and blocking its operations with the international banking institutions of which we form a part; and by creating difficulties for us in the mining and trade of copper, our principal wealth, with litigations against us by a multinational corporation in several countries.

He concluded, with an eye on events that promised an eruption of violence in Chile:

The opposition and the government's parties must realize that the President of the Republic will use all the means in his power to avoid violence, and any sector that tries to unleash it will run head-on into the decision of the executive branch to stop this country from reaching a confrontation. I have said it before and I repeat it again with a full sense of the higher responsibilities given to me: as long as I am President I shall avoid, I shall prevent it. That is how I must defend Chile and the revolutionary process we are living through.

This is what I have pledged before history and before my conscience, and I shall keep this pledge. This gives me the authority — because my two years and several months of office prove that I carry out my word — to ask the democratic opposition (since I know that the rest of the opposition will not listen to reason and will never understand what is best for Chile) to understand this: the course of history cannot be stopped, nations do not move backwards, social injustice cannot endure, and man rightfully longs to develop his whole personality. It will have to understand that countries like ours, in the process of development, are still strongly affected by the drama of millions of our fellowmen who live in other countries with the same characteristics as ours: hunger, illiteracy, unemployment, total lack of rest and recreation. . . .

No country has so far succeeded in organizing a new society in the ways we have chosen to do it. And we are doing it, in spite of the hardships that so often block our way. . . .

A few days before the new cabinet was to be formed in Chile, Washington had decided to give its Chile policy a new twist. The most serious hardships in the history of Chile were about to confront us openly.

10

Like the Chilean reactionaries, the U. S. government believed that the
parliamentary elections on March 4, 1973, would permit the legal "overthrow" of Allende. The imperialists generally trust the practical know-
how of their allies in our country. This time, they repeated their error
of 1970.

The March 4 results came as a shock to Washington. They showed that
the popular conscience in Chile could withstand the maneuvers of the
United States, in complicity with the Chilean reactionaries, and would
not be bullied by the strong economic measures or the political and ideological manipulation of the United States, even when it used sophisticated methods of social psychology against Chile. On the contrary, the
elections proved that the capacity to mobilize the masses had been growing, and that the people's emergent power could serve as a base for
revolutionary government.

The United States saw the final objective of their Chilean policy go
down the drain once more. The methods tried between November 1970
and March 1973 had proved fruitless, and the Popular Unity government
had not been overthrown. There was only one thing to do: change
course and use the toughest method of intervention, resorting to an
outright conspiracy by supporting the military coup, with the Pentagon
in league with Chile's military.

This possibility had been considered in the program of action approved in November 1970, and many American actions during the past
two and a half years had been in gradual preparation for this opportunity.

125

As part of this preparation, for example, the United States had maintained and increased its special relations with Chile's armed forces, its personal contacts with some of their officers, its financial support and political directives to groups of the far right — like "Fatherland and Liberty" — and the reinforcement of their paramilitary character; in addition, there were the increase in terrorist activities by the right wing, the establishment of secret intelligence networks within the country, the large quantity and type of armaments supplied to the different armed forces and the measures of economic interference and diplomatic strangulation, which had failed to obtain the final objective, but which could contribute to its success if that objective were sought by means of armed intervention. The atmosphere for crisis was prepared and would be used as a pretext for the hired assassins to bring off the coup d'etat.

 In the three weeks following March 4, matters took an abrupt turn in the White House. The decision to carry out the plan conceived by the Pentagon in 1970 could only be made at the highest level. And it was.

What were the characteristics of the Pentagon's plan?

I. The agency responsible for American intervention in Chile is the Defense Intelligence Agency, working mainly through Naval Intelligence. It coordinates the execution of the plan of action against Chile, receiving information processed by other intelligence services and departments of the American government, including the CIA, whose director supervises all such operations. The whole thing is directed by the National Security Council, headed by the President and implemented by the President's security advisor.

Why the Naval Intelligence Agency? Because the Chilean Navy is more conservative than the rest of the armed forces; also because the plan (its general strategy will be described below) could easily be carried out in conjunction with the Chile-United States naval maneuvers, Operation Unitas, which would permit the presence of American warships in Chilean waters and ports, bringing technical equipment and specialists; immediate logistical cooperation could come directly from the American ships; and their presence alone would be a persuasive factor for the seditious Chilean military and a potential armed threat to the people of Chile and to its political forces.

II. The best time to implement this plan is September, when Operation Unitas is carried out each year. All the Chilean armed forces are then in top condition in terms of training discipline; they are prepared for war and tuned up for the only joint action in which they participate together each year: the military parade on September 19, Army Day, and on the twentieth, Independence Day. Beginning in August, the land, sea, and air forces are kept on their bases and undergo rigorous training; the chain of command reinforces itself, allowing superiors to cooperate without rivalry in the training of officers, noncommissioned officers, and enlisted men. And finally, during this month, the annual contingents of draftees have already been in the service long enough to be adapted to it, so that those who are politically "suspect" (likely to refuse to participate in sedition) may be identified and disarmed.

III. The subversive action of the Chilean military is supported not only by and from the American ships of the Unitas maneuvers, but also by the presence, before and during the maneuvers, of at least one hundred officers, noncommissioned officers, and others highly specialized in various tasks (logistics, electronics, communications, sabotage, secret intelligence, and the like) that are necessary to the complete objective of the plan which appears in point V of this report. All those officers (including a few commanders, several dozen lieutenant commanders, lieutenants, and lieutenants junior grade) noncommissioned officers and assistants do not have to be in Chile at the same time. Some go for a short stopover; others make several trips — depending on their duties — returning to the United States or moving on to other Latin American countries where they establish contact with other American or local groups; still others must stay on until the coup itself. Preparations for Operation Unitas and other ceremonies connected with it give these naval personnel a legitimate excuse for being there. They also justify the frequent comings and goings to and from the country, and they explain the interviews with the authorities, the middle- and low-ranking officers of all the armed forces, and even with the Cuerpo de Carabineros. Naturally, the purpose of their presence will be known to only a very few of their Chilean colleagues; it is better for them to know it only indirectly, so that the institutional "susceptibility" of the armed forces does not interfere with the plans being carried out.

IV. The objectives of the plan and the need for active participation of American personnel call for a critical appraisal of Chile's armed forces by the U. S. government. Here is the Pentagon's appraisal:
    a. There is a lack of institutional cohesion among the four branches of the Chilean armed forces — the army, navy, air force and carabineros — which makes it difficult for them to work together, except on plans for the possibility of foreign war. Chile has not been at war with a for-

eign power in ninety years; although they are regularly revised, these
plans have not been tested. On the other hand, there is constant evidence of professional jealousy between the different branches and even
between sectors of the same branch. Even the fundamental question of
the control of military air equipment (whether it is to be concentrated
in the Air Force or whether there is to be a naval air force and air equipment or light aircraft, helicopters, etc., for the Carabineros and the
Army) has not definitely been settled, in spite of recent developments.

b. Each of the armed services has a different political role and its
own historical tradition. Their respective military "doctrines" corre-
spond to different schools of thought and differ on key points. The
same thing goes for their "ideologies" and their latent political attitudes.
These ideologies vary in their attitudes toward the interests of U. S.
security in the hemisphere and in the world, and they sometimes clash.
The dependence of each branch on the United States for supplies of
armaments, equipments, and so forth, varies. That is why there is need
for direct participation of U. S. personnel in a joint operation of the
Chilean armed forces, who have key contacts there — officers formed
and indoctrinated in the United States — who can be fully trusted. The
Pentagon does not have faith in the viability or the efficiency of the so-
called National Objective elaborated by the Chilean armed forces. The
United States must instill or impose cohesion upon them, persuading
or forcing them to accept it as their true national objective.

c. We must consider the possibility of a political rift between the
chiefs of staff of the armed forces in situations of legal, social, economic,
or political crisis. It is an argument that supports the preceding one.

d. The four armed services are basically incapable of running themselves as institutions; this is especially evident in the Army and the Air
Force. Although the professional level of the officers and noncommissioned officers, as well as their personal qualities, is sometimes
satisfactory and even good, each branch of the service lacks the minimal
methods and modern practices necessary to run smoothly. The very
autonomy of each branch aggravates the situation. In Washington one
can see examples of this every day in the archaic and inefficient handling
of funds for military purchases from the United States. This ineffi-
ciency could only be greater when there is a takeover of power, with
all its consequences; that is, when it involves running the entire country, including the difficult administration of the economy, particularly
its foreign trade. One more reason for U. S. aid in these extreme
circumstances.

e. Chile's armed services, with their yearly quota of draftees, reflect, on a certain scale, the general characteristics of the country's social phenomenon: the jealousies and hostilities between the classes, the class struggle. This puts obstacles in the way of those officers determined to confront Marxism, for they cannot be absolutely sure of anyone in the various corps, neither officers, noncommissioned officers, nor enlisted men, neither career men nor conscripts. They cannot act effectively alone; they need the United States.

f. The general situation of the country, divided socially and politically by the class struggle between workers, intellectuals, and others has repercussions in the armed forces, where it paralyzes, up to a point, the decision of those officers determined to act. They are afraid of the reaction of the masses in the unions and elsewhere; they need the United States to give them psychological security and encouragement to act.

g. Finally, the Chilean armed forces alone do not have the proper technology to carry off a coup d'etat with the sophisticated, rapid, and efficient methods Chile's case demands. Therefore, U. S. military assistance is indispensable and decisive.

V. The objectives of the plan are the following. In the first place, all means of communication within the country must be cut off and disrupted; at the same time, all of Chile must be isolated from the outside world for as long as it is necessary. In this context, "cutting off communications" is used in its widest sense: it is not limited to the usual communications — telephone, telegraph, highways, railroads, air transport — but includes, as well, control of all paths of communication for decisions, information, and instructions between the highest administrative, economic, political (with special attention to the left wing parties), and union officials. The entire structure of the country must be pulled apart quickly and simultaneously; no system of power — especially the state or the administration, political parties, unions, or other organizations — must be allowed to reorganize its decision-making line of command or its discipline. Whole cities, regions, or provinces and districts, industrial sectors, universities, factories, offices, and other sensitive areas will be isolated from the rest of the country and from each other. This first objective paralyzes all decision-making centers of power, so that the second and third objectives will be successful.

The second objective consists in allowing only one coordinated center of decision and control to exist: the armed forces, which will

carry out the coup, and their collaborators — Chilean civilians and U. S.
military personnel. Naturally, the American embassy must be allowed
to move freely and to keep communications open with the outside
world; and all possible efforts will be made to slow down or block similar activities in other embassies and official organizations representing
other foreign countries in Chile. (It may be convenient, under certain
circumstances, to allow such groups — as well as newspapermen, priests,
etc. — occasionally to witness some of the consequences of the coup
and to pass on the results to the enemy both within the borders of the
country and outside, so that the general paralysis of the country will
increase, and the inaction and confusion abroad will continue for as
long as possible.) This way, total power over the country (both negative and positive) can be controlled from one decision-making center;
and this can be done even if there is resistance to the coup by armed
or unarmed sectors. The success of this operation — and its subsequent
effects, which will benefit U. S. interests in Chile, in the hemisphere and
in the rest of the world — is assured by this single center of control
formed by the armed forces involved in the coup (with plenty of technical, strategic, and economic support); and even more by the fact that,
whether they are well informed about the original plan or have only a
vague idea of its nature, they have carried it out thanks to a "know-how"
that is superior to the enemy's and even surpasses the armed forces' own
capacity.

The third objective of the plan, once the enemies are isolated and
their organizations have been broken up, is to quickly identify, track
down, and eliminate them. In the early stages of the operation — which
will undoubtedly require intense military force and perhaps, in certain
cases, the use of heavy arms and many risks — the casualties suffered by
the engaged troops will draw them closer together, making it easier for
them to act as a tight and disciplined unit, and spurring them on without
pity for the enemy. They will destroy the most dangerous enemies
more efficiently; allowance must be made for the fact that we cannot
protect the "innocents," a regrettable situation, but one that does present certain advantages relative to the fourth objective. The first
enemies that must be eliminated are the high-ranking commanders,
officers, noncommissioned officers, regular enlisted men, and draftees
who oppose this action. From the beginning it will be evident who is
in favor and who opposed, by the way in which they perform the
duties forced on them by the fighting, making it possible to eliminate
those who seem to be against it and to integrate those in favor, involving them in volunteer missions. In the beginning, a small number of

trusted officers, who are fully or at least partially aware of the plans, can do a good psychological job by influencing attitudes and behavior in the course of the fighting; eventually, this useful work can be passed on to other officers and noncoms, thus forcing them to become increasingly involved, although they may not even have partial knowledge of the general plan and its objectives.

The fourth objective is to spread psychological terror and, if necessary, to control physical resistance through military efforts, using light and heavy weapons; to concentrate all power in one decision-making center made up of the anticommunist armed forces and their friends inside the country and abroad; and lastly, to place a tight control over all means of communication in Chile. (This last sows confusion among the enemy and its potential supporters at home and abroad, whether they be foreigners, or their own representatives in other countries, or organizations, etc.) The climate so created will insure the power of the state and will permit it to rebuild its entire apparatus — its administration, the public and private economy — to conform with the wishes of the United States and to satisfy the Chilean military and other nationalist (sic) forces. While carrying out this fourth objective, the spread of fear among the hostile or indifferent civilian masses must coincide with a bolstering of confidence on the part of the armed forces, in themselves, in the United States, and in other friends. This terror is necessary; without it certain elements in the Chilean military might not have enough confidence in their rights and in their power.

The last objective and strategy of the plan is to establish a government friendly to the United States, indebted to it for its origin, and dependent on it for its future needs; a government that will possess full military, economic, and political power, and that will enjoy the prestige that success brings with it; a government that will guarantee the national security interests of the United States and the Western world, and that will protect American citizens and their private interests; a government that can be reasonably sure it will remain in power, having won its stability through a sweeping and efficient use of force; a government that has definitely eliminated any dangerous persons and organizations that may have opposed, with good chance of success, the interests of the United States and the real interests of Chile (sic) at home and abroad.

VI. The means used by the United States to carry out their share of the plan are the following:

The first means is the existence of the plan itself. This may sound like a paradox. It is not. The inability of the Chilean armed forces to accomplish on their own the proposed objectives explains it: the preparation of this plan, its dissemination among the Chilean officers, and especially the first stages of its implementation are a real exercise in coordination between the officers themselves, between the officers and Chilean civilians who collaborate decisively in these operations, and, significantly, between the officers and authorities and specialists from the Pentagon and other American agencies. This coordination is itself a technical and a political means indispensable in carrying out the plan.

The second means is to adapt this plan into the overall scheme of action of the U. S. Government's policy toward Chile: including "overt" (public) political, economic, financial, and armament-supply programs, as well as "covert" (secret) intelligence operations in these same areas and others. In other words, the present plan constitutes the main hypothesis for the uninterrupted course of action — which is the United States' general policy — to solve the Chilean dilemma. Although the other programs recently proposed have their own independent objectives (for example, to block credits and check any ambitions for revolutionary reforms or special relations with other foreign countries), in terms of the main plan, it signifies that conditions in and outside the country must "ripen" in order to make the present plan progressively viable.

The second means, then, is to fit this plan into the overall scheme of plans and programs for action that constitutes the United States' general policy toward Chile; in this framework, all the other actions help to "ripen" the conditions that will make possible the action foreseen in the main hypothesis — the decisive action which characterizes the present plan.

The third means consists of a series of specific interlocking actions coordinated by the agency (U.S. naval intelligence services) that puts the plan into effect. The most important of these are:

1. The presence of the U. S. Navy's Unitas ships in territorial waters or at sea near the coast, or even in Chilean ports (at the same time doing everything possible to conceal from other countries America's role in the plan, which could be suggested by the presence of this fleet in a port like Valparaiso); the ships are there to give psychological support and to assist with strategy, communications, and even more directly with electronic and other technical equipment.

2. The presence on land, using the Unitas maneuvers as a pretext, of an adequate number (approximately one hundred) of American military

and civilian experts, professionally qualified and highly trained in cutting off communications, special sabotage, the breaking down of administrative organization, secret intelligence, and directing strategy and operations; they would include antiguerrilla experts and so forth.

3. Direct logistic assistance, which can be given ahead of time and openly through the regular programs for the purchase of armaments and equipment from the United States, by the Navy and the rest of the armed forces, and through the usual military aid programs; this assistance is to be intensified shortly before the action, and completed by accelerated secret supply operations and logistic aid, at the country's borders and on the coast, by means of air and land bridges, using Chilean civilians as go-betweens.

4. Assistance with technology and equipment through the same channels and in the same conditions as in point 3.

5. Direct and indirect help in the centralization and coordination of plans for each action and each stage of the operations. (This can be done in Chile, in neighboring countries, or in the United States itself through direct contacts with Chilean officers and civilians, and by organizing, with this in mind, a closed communications system at decisive moments.)

6. Economic and financial aid.

7. Help from police experts, through training given ahead of time and through the actual presence of American specialists in Chile before, during, and after the coup.

8. Rigging and manipulating information within the country, as well as that coming in and going out, during the entire critical period. (This action will be considered essential to cut off communications in the broad sense mentioned above, and requires special attention; thus, various sets of information on events, with alternative versions, are prepared (for distribution when the right time comes) long before these events take place to permit the news to get out fast — sometimes even ahead of time, to provoke the confusion, uncertainty, disorganization, isolation, and terror that make it easy to eliminate enemies and to annihilate all chances of resistance as quickly as possible.

9. The methods intended to create physical and psychological paralysis within the country and confusion abroad, summed up in the word "terror," can constitute the last reference to the specific means of action listed as examples in this section.

This was the plan prepared by the United States government in the first half of 1970; it was to be applied in Chile as a countermeasure to the expected victory of the people and their representative Salvador Allende. In this summary — which is not exhaustive and does not pretend to reproduce American documents word for word — we can see the shaping of events that, today, have become brutal fact.

The Chilean government noticed the change in policy that had taken place in Washington. In March and April 1973, after making a preliminary study of relations between the United States and Chile, Salvador Allende seemed very concerned. In his April 10 speech before the Asamblea Sindical Mundial (Assembly of World Labor Unions), he denounced the direct interference and subversive acts of the United States in Chile. The exposure of the ITT plot at the Senate hearings gave clear proof of this. Private conversations with him on March 26 and 27, and again on April 10, confirmed this preoccupation. "I need more time," was his refrain. Direct intervention by the United States seemed inevitable to him, and he was trying to delay it as much as possible. He would have to count on the strength of the people, ever on their guard against those who tried to provoke them into rash violence, and on their capacity to paralyze the country's economy, as a force to stave off the threat gathering over Chile. His reference to this violence in his speech of March 27 reveals his concern.

In planning his policy for the rest of 1973, President Allende had to consider the battle he faced on two fronts: against the right wing and against imperialism. On the former, he could use his political skill; his margin of action was limited, but at least he could determine it. On the other front, he faced a force that could not be measured; the American decision to destroy Chile depended on circumstances that a government of a country like Chile could not change or really know enough about. It was impossible to know ahead of time exactly when or how such a decision would go into effect. For the United States, Chile's example could have global repercussions, and Washington's motives for acting at any one given moment and in a specific manner could very well have nothing to do with Chile, but could depend instead on American interests in some other part of the world, within the framework of its global strategy.

In March and April, in Washington, two series of events took place that showed the importance of the decision made by the Nixon administration and the nature of its future policy toward Chile.

One of them was the turn taken by the Senate hearings on ITT's plot in Chile. Besides shedding new light on the actions of that multinational corporation, they showed that the American government had taken a much more active part in it than anyone had been able to prove until then. But the most serious thing about all this was the United States' readiness to bring it out into the open. This phenomenon began to appear in the first sessions held by Senator Frank Church's subcommittee. The senators and the staff conducting the investigation threw themselves into their work, yet they were constantly upstaged by the ease with which U. S. government officials — who had held their posts during the period in which the events exposed at the hearings had occurred, and most of whom still held them in 1973 — admitted the government's participation in the acts of intervention, with all the details relating to the circumstances, and sometimes even contradicting themselves. This was frankly amazing. The U. S. government had never admitted this kind of intervention in a country with which it had diplomatic relations, except when the circumstances justified, in its eyes, a serious and long drawn-out major intervention in the internal affairs of that country. Naturally, one could maintain that these revelations showed the "openness" of American society and the strength of institutions like the Senate. But this argument, which can be refuted in several ways, became laughable when, for the first time in the history of the U. S. Senate, a member of the CIA, William Broe, testified publicly before the subcommittee, so that everybody could know what he said. The executive branch had given authorization to both Broe and the CIA. This was unprecedented. The executive branch could have demanded — as it always had in the history of its relations with Congress — that the CIA's disclosures take place behind closed doors. This demand was not made.

The Nixon administration had authorized Broe's public testimony, which seriously involved it in clandestine acts of economic aggression, as well as subversion, within another country; this was against all principles officially proclaimed by the United States, and violated the basic principles for relations between sovereign states, the United Nations charter, and all the commitments that existed in the international community and between the United States and Chile. The American government was thus making it easy for definite proof of its illegal involvements in Chile to be presented, for which some of its other officials' testimony had opened the way. When a government authorizes anything of the

kind in a matter so delicate, it is because it *wants* to make the facts
known. Not only was Broe authorized to do what he did, but he was
actually carrying out instructions from the Nixon administration to
testify before the Senate. The United States was officially letting it be
known that it had taken part in acts to overthrow a legitimate foreign
government, to inform all those concerned — the Chilean government,
the Third World countries, whether they were friendly to Chile or not,
particularly those in Western Europe and Latin America, and the Chilean opposition above all — that the United States was prepared to bring
down Salvador Allende's administration. The revelation of its recent
acts of intervention in Chile served to announce its decision, made a
few days before, to use every means within its reach to intervene in
Chile until it gained its objective. Thus, aside from the intentions of the
American senators, the exposure of the ITT plot showed that there was
another that was much more serious: the U. S. government's wide-open
plot to destroy Chile, which was to be carried out in full view this time,
without any "errors" of judgment (like those committed by ITT and
the government itself) and which was to employ the right means to attain
the objective it had set its sights on.

Another event that helped unmask the official decision made in
March was the opening, that same month, of the second round of
Chile-United States talks in Washington. This, you will recall, had
been prearranged the year before. As far as the United States was
concerned, the purpose of these talks had already been carefully
analyzed.

These conversations, which took place after the White House had
made its final decision, are unique. An oppressive atmosphere hovered
around the Chilean participants: Ambassador Letelier, Deputy Maira,
and others. Assistant Secretary Charles Meyer had already resigned
from his post. Jack Kubisch (who was recommended by Kissinger after
they met in Paris during the conversations with the Vietnamese) had
been appointed assistant secretary for Latin America, but he did not
take part in these talks; John Crimmins, his assistant, represented him.
(The latter appears often in the ITT memos, where his name is mis-
spelled "Crimmons" and his opinions are identified with Meyer's,
which is rather farfetched. In 1970, during a meeting of the Overseas
International Council to discuss the situation in Peru — sponsored that
year by Chicago's Adlai Stevenson Institute — Crimmins exploded and,
in his outburst, said, "Why do Latin Americans hate us so much, when
they know that our heart is pure?" and obtained this answer, "Your
heart is pure, but your hands are big.") Crimmins was accompanied by

Sidney Weintraub, former counselor in Chile, and at that time in charge
of economic affairs in the State Department. Thus, the atmosphere was
not very "diplomatic."

The Chilean proposal — bitterly debated within the Popular Unity
party because it was considered too favorable to the United States —
favored going back to the Treaty of 1914 "for the solution of any difficulties between the two countries and to assure the maintenance of
peace and good friendship between them." It was flatly turned down
by the U. S. delegates. By refusing to apply this important law, which
was both pertinent to the case and still in effect, the United States was
showing its intention to remain at loggerheads with Chile and not abide
by international law in solving their differences. But these premonitions
about the American decision in March were confirmed by John Crimmins's last words to the Chilean ambassador, offering three options
which apparently veiled an ultimatum: the two countries either freeze
the conflict, settle it, or else there would be war.[1]

Like Chile, the United States knew that such differences could not
be frozen, that they obey their own dynamics; therefore, the first choice,
at least, was false. By accepting it, Chile would give the United States a
free hand to step up its aggressions through the multinational corporations and in the arena of Third World countries. For the United States,
"settling the conflict" meant settling it in their own favor — that is,
through a partial agreement, imposed unilaterally, which, once accepted,
would turn back the Chilean revolution. In putting forward these options, the United States knew that neither freezing nor settling could
be accepted by it or by Chile. It was actually offering an ultimatum. It
proposed war.

That is how this second round of talks between Chile and the United
States ended in March. John Crimmins, the former American ambassador to the Dominican Republic, where he was appointed right after the
1965 invasion by the Marines, and where he worked with Counselor
Schlaudemann (the key man before, during, and after that intervention,
and the second in command at the embassy in Santiago under Korry and
his successor Ambassador Nathaniel Davis, who in turn had come from
Guatemala) had carried out his mission.

The Americans had laid their cards on the table. The moment for
intervention and the specific plan to be applied in Chile were only a
question of time and international circumstances that had little to do

with that country. The Chilean government foresaw this. On April 13, the foreign ministry prepared a study on the question. It read:

1. The United States has recently adopted a new policy toward Chile. It continues and replaces the one set by the National Security Council (with Nixon presiding and Kissinger directing) and proposed by the State Department in early November 1970.

2. The U. S. objective is the destruction of the Popular Unity government. The means it is now ready to use are more varied, less cautious, and more aggressive than during the period between the end of 1970 and the beginning of 1973. Nevertheless, this tougher policy does not exclude underground tactics or ambiguous and "invisible" ones that may prove more efficient than others, used at the same time, for the final U. S. objective. Nor does it exclude, at least in theory (when the menace becomes "real"), violent means and direct aggression, whether they be economic, political, or diplomatic.

3. The failure to pay "sufficient" (or even "symbolic") indemnification for the nationalization of copper is not the only reason behind this definite and all-out U. S. policy against Chile. This country's decision not to indemnify the nationalized firms affects many private American interests, just as it affects a key principle of the imperialist system of the capitalist multinational monopolies of which the United States is the center; but, far beyond this, the decision affects the general foundations of the system itself and the security of the United States. This is true because, first, the very existence and actions of the Chilean government are damaging to U. S. national interests in Chile, and secondly, its example can have great influence on power relations in Latin America and on the Third World in general; but even more than that, because the success of the Chilean experience has a very important effect on power relations essential to the United States in its dealings with industrialized countries in the West, such as France and Italy. The possible success of the Chilean experience cannot be accepted by the United States. Its accomplishment and its solidity can be a serious setback for U. S. power and prestige in its major relations with the great powers, and can harm its global plan (underway during the past two years) to set up a new world order favorable to the imperialist system and to the United States as its dominant power. In this sense Chile succeeds Vietnam, in a way, as another borderline case (Pham Van Dong made this serious observation at the end of 1971), principally because, as international examples of

the fight against imperialism, the wars of national liberation have
not had the real effect that the Chilean experience (the peaceful
road to socialism and the strategic alliance between Marxists and
Christians, etc.) has today in reinforcing and extending anti-
imperialist action in the world. In short, the failure to indemnify
(add to this the decay of the principle of compensation) is not the
only thing that worries the United States. It is the existence of a
government like Popular Unity, which is capable of acts like non-
payment of indemnification for copper; and, going even further,
it is the existence of a country like Chile where a government of
the People's Union exists and endures.

4. The tactics the United States is apparently about to put into
practice include the following:
   a. Political and diplomatic decisions (both private and public)
that will mislead the Chilean government about the real objectives
of U. S. policy and the methods it will use to carry it out. This
will slow down our reactions or confuse us, causing us to react late
and only partially, instead of starting an international offensive to
fortify our position and interfere with or prevent the success of
American policy. Or else it will have effects that are even worse:
for instance, Chile may misjudge real U. S. intentions and adopt a
mistaken policy, or fail to adopt one at the decisive moment when
the United States launches its own; or lastly, Chile may make a
wrong or only partial or contradictory move.
   b. Specific actions or the exploitation of circumstances that put
the Chilean government in an ambiguous, doubtful, or weak position (vis à vis imperialism) in order to stir up dissension in Popular
Unity and the Left, creating subsequent political problems for the
government.
   c. Other specific actions or the exploitation of situations intensifying the opposition's attacks on the government of Chile, by
bringing to light events that involve individuals, parties, or other
opposition groups, directly or indirectly, making them suspect (if
not guilty) of complicity with the United States; this would set
off a campaign of accusations and counteraccusations with subsequent antagonisms, tensions, and polarization.
   d. Stepping up the economic blockade with actions that become more visible and eventually come out into the open; this
growing threat will create uncertainty and partial, hasty, or in-
appropriate decisions in the government, and will hurt the
country's economy and its foreign trade.
   e. Financial and economic decisions of international importance that directly, or by their effects on the market and banking

centers in the West, will make it extremely difficult for Chile to
get credit, to prolong or favorably readjust the payment of its
foreign debts, or to obtain good prices and conditions for either
its exports or its imports. (In either case, this type of action can
concentrate on markets or products that are decisive for Chile's
economy or that influence the government's policies — that is,
in areas where these actions would do the most damage, socially
and politically.) These difficulties, limitations, or distortions will
affect national and international transportation, technological
exchanges, the running of the country's industrial apparatus, the
basic supply of consumer goods, and so forth.

f. Covert or overt political pressures, applied through statements or diplomatic memorandums discussing U. S. policy toward
Chile, to persuade Western countries with which Chile has more or
less satisfactory bilateral relations to break these off and to thus
stop Chile from making the most of secondary (not antagonistic)
contradictions in the capitalistic system.

g. An increase in actions and forms of aggression (including
embargoes and the like, but using channels that bypass the juridi-
cal-political channels) in Third World countries, mainly in the
West — but possibly extending into other countries of the Third
World, as well as to multilateral organizations. Perhaps the
American government will even take up the defense of private
interests, openly transforming the conflict between these interests and Chile into a conflict between governments (as a warning
to Third World countries and to American public opinion that
actions like Chile's are matters of state in the eyes of the United
States).

h. The preceding actions and others will be used — through
open intervention or through bilateral or diplomatic messages, and
so forth — to notify every country, whether or not they are at
odds with the United States, that Chile is a real danger that it will
not condone, a threat to its interests (and, going to extremes, a
threat to its security, depending on how the situation develops).
In this way, it will try to stop any growing relations between Chile
and other nations, isolating this country and blocking its international political attempts to defend itself against U. S. aggression
and its political and diplomatic efforts to swing the conflict in its
favor or to win friends.

(NOTE: This is not an exhaustive list of possible American
tactics, and it does not imply that the United States will use each
of these methods or use them simultaneously; but it is important
to make it clear that the United States has already openly started
some of these actions, that there are indications that others will

follow, and that those pointed out above are at least plausible
and have many precedents.)

5. The facts, proofs, and indications on which the entire analysis
is based are very varied and complex. Many of them have been
going on since 1970. Some of the most notorious of these
occurred in the last few months. We must also take into account
a number of decisive events of a political, social, and economic
nature that have occurred in both countries. In Chile, for example,
they include the confrontation in October, the attitude of the
armed forces, the March elections. In the United States, also
during the last few months, there has been Nixon's reelection
with more than 60 percent of the votes; the results of its foreign
policy in Indochina, Europe, Japan, the Middle East, and vis à vis
China and the USSR; and in domestic policy, the concentration
of the Executive's power, the weakening of the Republican and
Democratic parties and of dissenting political and social groups.
The respective internal situations of the two countries have objectively prepared the way for this new American policy, and,
from the U. S. point of view, have set up the need for it; at the
same time, they have made possible the use of tactics and methods
like those described above. But aside from this, we can mention
as examples a number of recent events that today, April 13, 1973,
stand up as sufficient proof and indication to make the above
analysis completely valid.
   a. The results of the conversations in March. To be precise,
the *impasse* (notwithstanding the later contrary explanations of
American representatives, that are of the type described in point
(*a*) of section 4, and are therefore misleading) *with an ultimatum*
—since the presentation of three alternatives is an authentic and
serious ultimatum that puts Chile in the following situation:
(*1*) The United States *defines* (or dictates) the only possible policies (according to it) between the two countries; (*2*) the three
choices are presented as the *only ones* possible, all others being
excluded by the United States, especially the plans presented by
Chile during these conversations, as well as any previous agreements adopted between the two countries, or others that might
eventually arise in the future, or still others that have precedents
in Third World countries; (*3*) each of these three alternatives (and
the United States knows this) is unacceptable, or even impossible,
for the government of Chile. In short:
   —One alternative is unacceptable because it implies an essential change in the nature of the Popular Unity government that
would have incalculable consequences both internal — in the heart

of the Popular Government itself and of the left wing, as well as on the cohesion of the political forces or by its moral, psychological, social, economic or other effects — and external — the success of the Chilean experience, its viability as an instrument in the fight against imperialism, and its value as an example for the rest of the world would be seriously affected; add to this the deterioration of Chile's prestige and influence, which would be hit hard by this choice. Another aggravating factor: the choice of this alternative would lead to an "agreement" — regardless of the sum involved — on the indemnification of the copper companies and on the principle of compensation as well, with the United States using this policy to destroy everything the Popular Unity government stands for; because imperialism actually has to prove to the world that a government capable of nationalizing copper without indemnification should not survive unless it makes radical changes, for example, in its behavior toward the United States, as we said in section 3.

—A second alternative (a "ratified" conflict that would, theoretically, be frozen in actual terms) cannot be accepted by Chile (and the United States knows it), first, because it is inconceivable in an international perspective — nowadays we cannot freeze relations between two countries with so many conflicting interests that are fundamental to each; secondly, because the development of internal events in Chile necessarily places in the near future the additional conditions that would break up the "freeze" and, on the other hand, because private American interests affected by events in Chile cannot be "frozen" on the say-so of the United States alone; third, "agreeing on" or "regulating" the conflict can create dissension between the Popular Unity administration and the Left; fourth, the actual terms of the conflict, which would be "frozen," already imply serious harm to Chile's economy and other sectors that would eventually worsen; and finally, because keeping the conflict at a standstill under the existing terms really means putting Chile's interests "on ice," paralyzing its defenses against imperialism, and gradually isolating the country. None of this is even imaginable without a "guarantee pact" involving one or more foreign powers, all of which would place Chile at the mercy of the United States or in a subordinate international position with respect to Third World countries.

—A third alternative (definite rupture) naturally contains an important threat, which pinpoints the nature of the ultimatum within the overall American strategy planned since March; this should be analyzed carefully, because the United States is actually proposing that, in this case, there would be no holds barred and that the fight would be to the finish.

Conclusion: the United States warns Chile, in Washington, that
its present objectives expect Chile to adapt its domestic and international policies to those of the United States, under conditions
that are contrary to the official nature and objectives of the Chilean
government, the stability of the country, and its basic interests;
the United States thus makes it clear that it will not tolerate the
present situation in Chile, which is a threat to its own security and
to its national and global interests. Yet the apparent ambiguity of
leaving three alternatives open — thus possibly leading one to believe that American policy toward Chile is not very rigid or hard,
or that Chile has time in its favor — is not inconsistent with all the
declarations of the U. S. representatives, news commentaries, and
so forth, that the talks between the two countries are not yet
closed; for one of the best known tactics of imperialism is to sow
uncertainty in the Chilean government in order to keep it from
reacting in its own defense against this new policy and to neutral-
ize any political or diplomatic offensive launched internationally
by Chile in an effort to accumulate "confrontation power" (which
can even turn into bargaining power favorable to Chile) — that
is, to put Chile in a position where it cannot become an international or national "dissuasive power" to stop imperialism from
carrying any further its policy to destroy Chile.

b. The second element that backs up this whole analysis is the
nature of the disclosures of the ITT plot, those made public at
the Senate hearings as well as those let out by the news media as
leaks. It is not that the Senate committee investigating ITT was
deliberately set up to make the disclosures and act as a vehicle for
American policy against Chile; what is remarkable is that such
serious revelations were permitted at this investigation, that the
American President "consented" to let some of his officials con-
fess all kinds of unscrupulous aggressions by the United States
against Chile. These were unprecedented acts that were carried
out not as a result of a set of circumstances and links or because
some of Nixon's political enemies wanted the investigation. The
Nixon administration took off its political mask to show that,
not so long ago, it had repeatedly attacked the government of a
country with which it had friendly relations, without punishing
the agents responsible for these actions or even denying its own
guilt; the actors — agents or victims — had not changed at all.
Not even in the case of the "Pentagon papers" had the government's position been so seriously compromised internationally;
for, in that affair, the actors and the agents responsible had all
disappeared from the government, and the Johnson administration
had been replaced by Nixon's. The "confessions" at the Senate

hearings and the "leaks" of the news media are, in a way, like
those cases in which the United States has publicly assumed responsibility for its acts of aggression and armed intervention. There is
no doubt that the American executive branch and the leading
economic interests, as well as the multinational corporations,
could have prevented disclosure of a good number of these actions, for which the government was openly held answerable (for
example, the hearings could have been held in executive or secret
sessions); or, if these could not have been prevented, at least they
could have agreed on what was to be disclosed, covering up the
government's responsibility. In short, the American government
wanted to declare itself publicly responsible for these acts,
deliberately revealing that, as far as it was concerned, the situation in Chile was unacceptable and that its policy toward the
Popular Unity administration was defined and would not change.
The conspiracy against Chile was revealed not so much by the
ITT plot exposed in Washington, but by the fact that the American government allowed its responsibility in the direct aggression
against Chile to be publicly made known.

 c. The third known element that supports this analysis is the
decision of the U. S. government to sell its reserves of valuable and
strategic minerals, even if it was only a bluff, since the United
States was actually threatening to step up its attack on the vital
elements of Chile's economy — the marketing and the price of
copper — as is shown by certain characteristics that the copper
lawsuits have assumed in certain Western countries.

This same month, a report of the situation was taken to President Allende,
who, during the conversation on April 10 already mentioned, had made it
clear that he saw these acts coming; he said that he needed time to coun-
teract, that nothing much could be done against a determined world
power, and that it was difficult to know when or how it would go into
action; but that the government would do everything in its power to
defend Chile's sovereignty. The report (which proposed a foreign policy
designed to help gain time and objectively persuade the United States
and its allies, the Chilean reactionaries, to stop their aggression) began:

 The United States is adopting a tougher policy toward Chile.
It is determined not to let us gain any time in our fight against it.
From now until July (Paris Club meeting), the United States will
concretize its policy. Last March (at the Washington conversations) they gave us an ultimatum with no way out. The ultimatum
offered us three alternatives (agreement on indemnification;
freezing the conflict; and a definite rupture). They were pre-

sented in such terms that Chile could not accept any of them,
and the United States knew this. That makes them an ultimatum.
The United States would have us believe that the question of
indemnification and the application of the international principle
on which it should be based are responsible for its quarrel with
Chile. Nothing could be further from the truth. The double issue
of the copper and the international agreement on compensation
only serves to cover up the main conflict between the United
States and Chile. What the United States cannot accept is the
existence of a government like Popular Unity that can decide to
nationalize without indemnification, using legal methods that
paralyze the U. S. capacity to respond or at least limit it substantially. The international effect, in Latin America and the
Third World, of the persistence of the *via Chilena* causes problems
for the United States that are much more serious than the value
of the copper compensations, and even more serious than the
damage to the U. S. international principle that nationalizations
must be indemnified. After all, the mere survival (and, even more,
the success) of the Popular Unity government has a strong influence in countries like France and Italy, those areas of the world
that are vital to the basic and strategic interests of the United
States. That is how Kissinger saw it in September 1970, as we
have seen (background briefings in Chicago on September 16,
1970).

Consequently, the United States cannot relax its objective of
letting President Allende's administration deteriorate until it
falls completely apart. Only if Chile were to yield on the copper
question in such a way that the nature of the Chilean experiment
would be modified, would the United States consent to make the
question of copper the sole source of its conflict. But that is impossible. When the United States proposes freezing the conflict,
it sets a trap, trying to mislead us and throw us into confusion.
"Freezing" the conflict places us in a very ambiguous position
and limits Chile's chances of rallying international support. At the
same time, this solution does not eliminate the economic problems in Chile provoked by the United States. It demobilizes Popular Unity and the Chilean Left, it creates bad feeling among
them, and strengthens the position of the Right. In the meantime, the United States will continue to maneuver against us,
either directly (though not quite openly) or in such a way as to
wreck our relations with Western Europe and others.

In April the Chilean opposition launched its offensive. It is probable —
although the nature of the facts prevents proof — that the plan for this
offensive, which was very carefully conceived, relied on American ad-

vice. It was a propaganda campaign that did not stop at distorting the facts to provoke certain psychological repercussions in Chile and abroad. It made the most of every chance it had, and sparked off events like the brutal series of right wing terrorist acts, which it used to promote chaos in the country. Many of these acts, surrounded by mysterious circumstances, were blamed on American secret agents (for instance, the sensationally sadistic murder of a worker at a television station in Concepción.

One of the first things to spark off this campaign was the preliminary plan for the Escuela Nacional Unificada (Unified National School), which allowed the Right to mobilize students and parents, the Church, and above all, the armed forces. All the specific points brought out by the government to prove that it was a collective project, the official discussions, the democratic way in which it was taken up with the student and social organizations, and, finally, the high level sessions with those who, influenced by the propaganda campaign, had expressed their doubts (the Catholic hierarchy, the officers of the armed forces, the opposition itself) — all this could do nothing against the psychological and political manipulations used in this operation. The general lines of this preliminary plan for the ENU were drawn from UNESCO's recommendations on the subject, but this fact did not help either. The campaign led to demonstrations and street violence. Its purpose was precisely to create a climate of internal dissension and hatred, and to pave the way for acts of violence. At the end of April, a worker who demonstrated his support for the government was shot to death on the Alameda, Santiago's most important avenue. He was holding a book of poems by Pablo Neruda when he was killed. Many other victims paid with their lives. Those who had launched the campaign as a last resort could not have cared less; and those who were its instruments thought, often in good faith (this shows how successful the plan was), that they were defending values that were being threatened.

The right-wing magazine *Que Pasa* published an exhaustive report on the loss of human lives during the two and a half years of Allende's administration; it included quite a few who suffered heart attacks as a result of the strikes and the farmland expropriations. It listed casualties of terrorist acts without distinguishing between victims of the Right and the Left. The number of dead totalled almost one hundred. In the following months, the list of victims grew at an accelerated pace. There is no doubt that the terrorism during this period was almost exclusively the work of those who opposed the government; besides, only a small number of the victims who had been cited earlier by *Que Pasa* could be accounted for by crimes committed by the Left or by persons who supposedly belonged to the Left (remember the plan for terrorist provocations reported by ITT). And yet, even if we include all those murdered by the military during the attempted coup on June 29, the list of people killed for political reasons during the three years of Allende's administration, most of whom proved to be the victims of the government's enemies, totals probably not more than two hundred. How many zeros must be added to that as a result of the coup of September 11 and the first months of repression?

Beginning in May, the systematic terrorist attacks against the people and against Chile's industry spread throughout the whole country. Groups like "Fatherland and Liberty" vowed that these would be their political methods. Rightist representatives in Congress justified the use of arms in the streets. Allusions to the Djakarta massacre, which in previous years had appeared only as anonymous inscriptions written on walls, were resumed in the form of threats aimed by rightist members of Parliament directly at the left wing, spelling out the first and last names of the intended victims and adding, "Wait for Djakarta."

This terrorism was intended to build up a climate of fear. The psychological uncertainty spread by these acts among the less politically-conscious stratum of society, the middle class, exacerbated their worries about economic problems, which had been increased during this period by two factors: the intensified American economic blockade, whose effects were aggravated by measures effected outside the country to damage Chile's copper market; and the economic sabotage within the country, ranging from the operation of the black market to the hoarding of staple goods. A significant amount of liquid capital in the hands of the middle-class opposition was used in wild speculations that helped to distort the economic situation even more. This brief description obviously does not attempt to analyze this situation as a whole; it simply brings to light the subversive measures hatched by U. S. imperialism.

The "vicious circle they have built around us," of which Allende had spoken in March, was doing its best to make him break the pledge he had made "before history and before my conscience": to avoid violence.

The assassins picked their victims from among those who were close to Allende, to show the objectives of their terrorist campaign. They murdered the President's naval aide, Commander Arturo Araya, at night in his home. This was a warning not only to the government's partisans, but also to the Navy and the officers who remained loyal to their oath to respect the legitimate government of the Republic. The news media in the pay of the opposition — which proclaimed itself

seriously threatened by a government which, according to them, wanted
to suppress the media, since they were instrumental in forming public
opinion — tried, as usual, to blame the left wing for the assassination,
without success. The opposition was attempting to create small "Reichstag fires" and to find adequate "Van der Lübe."[2]

The propaganda outlets tried to mobilize women against the government; this scheme first was carried out at the end of 1971, following the
Brazilian model used at the time of the coup against Goulart — a procedure used at different times by European Fascists before seizing power.
Later on, this same maneuver was used systematically to provoke the
resignation of the Army's commander in chief, General Carlos Prats,
which, in the long run, set the stage for the coup d'etat by his successor,
Augusto Pinochet. First, General Prats was embroiled in menacing and
upsetting street incidents provoked by women; he was at his home with
President Allende when the wives of high-ranking military officers started
a demonstration outside, screaming in protest against the government and
the general.[3]

The news media were very important during this entire campaign. It
was not just a coincidence that ITT had advised President Nixon two
years earlier to subsidize the newspaper *El Mercurio*, the most important
spokesman for the opposition.

But the bloody incidents and, above all, the acts of violence initiated
by the armed forces, were even more important to the plan. Under the
pretext of searching for those who were breaking a law that had given
control of firearms to the military and prohibited the private possession
of weapons, some members of the armed forces, who had prepared their
plan and were carrying it out, used this law to start trouble in factories
and other work centers. They did not stop to search those who were
against the workers. And during these missions, which were generally
fruitless, they left many casualties. One such Air Force group opened
up graves in the Cimenterio General (Public Cemetery). All they found
were human remains; but people were painfully shocked by these incidents, the publicity lavished on them, and the terrible omens they
implied. It was an attempt to terrorize the workers, who were the base
of support for the government. The unsuccessful June 29 uprising,
which was a rehearsal for the coup on September 11, served this end as
well as others. There were many civilian casualties.

The participation of certain elements of the armed forces — most of
whom were ignorant of the plot, but were swept along by the actions
planned and set in motion by traitors working hand in hand with the
United States and its secret agents — was used to screen officers, non-

commissioned officers, and enlisted men and identify those who were
loyal to the constitutional government and would, therefore, be the
first victims when the coup broke out. For instance, in the months
following the aborted coup in June, in the Navy alone more than one
hundred men were harassed and persecuted. During this time, the per-
secutions were made to look legal, although illegal physical violence
was used. According to reports, they were shot without trial on the
day of the coup.

During this period, and after May, there were widespread trade-union
strikes. The trucks were once more paralyzed by order of their directing
committee, headed by León Vilamarin, who received instructions from
reactionary leaders of employers' organizations, in complicity with
American imperialism. The principal leader of those truckers who
were loyal to the government, and who stayed on the job, was assassi-
nated in the street. Those who headed the national organization for
the distribution of goods, equally linked to the reactionaries' organization, shut down their businesses, threatening the lives of those who
stayed open. The same thing happened in the liberal professional asso-
ciations, such as those of the doctors and lawyers. White-collar workers,
technicians, and some of the workers at El Teniente copper mine called
a work stoppage that lasted for several weeks, causing Chile enormous
losses in foreign currency. Most of the workers wanted to keep the
mines going.

The working class in general supported the government without
wavering. In spite of the seditious campaign, or rather against it, there
were complex and generous demonstrations of the growing strength of
Chile's social base. The "Cordones Industriales" and the Communal
Councils[4] illustrate this.

The country could not be set back, and the government would never
fall on its own.

The United States, which no longer even cared about saving appearances, still tried one last deceiving gesture. Perhaps it wanted to find out
the state of mind of the leaders in Santiago and their intentions. After
the bilateral conversations in March, some U. S. representatives had given
the impression that, as far as they were concerned, the talks were not
yet over.

Chile had had no ambassador in Washington since Orlando Letelier
had been called back to become foreign minister. The government had
wanted to send a successor immediately, but the Chilean Senate, which
must approve these appointments, refused to accept any of Salvador
Allende's choices for ambassador. Nothing like this had ever happened

in the history of Chile. Its embassies in Washington, Moscow, Paris, Havana, Prague, Hanoi, Pyongyang, some Middle East and other foreign capitals, had no ambassadors. According to the history of the Constitution, the theory behind the Senate's right to approve an ambassador was to make sure that he was qualified for the post; this right was not to be used as a political instrument against the government. But now, they were trying to cripple the country's foreign policy and break up its internal order.

When President Allende went to Argentina for the inauguration of its new President, during his last trip abroad, he saw Secretary of State Rogers. Rogers asked if he could visit Salvador Allende at the Chilean embassy. The President received him. This visit made no sense, and nothing resulted from it. Perhaps the United States still wanted Chile to believe that it was prepared to talk things over, while its intrigues were already making themselves felt. Anyway, it was doing its best to give the impression that its attitude toward Chile was normal. That was, in fact, the object of the visit, and of the hints that the conversations were still open. But the coup was the real end product of American policy.

Toward the end of August, the majority of the Chamber — members of the National Party, the Christian Democrats, and the rest of the reactionaries were all there — decided, in a gesture that had no constitutional weight, to denounce President Allende's "illegitimate" exercise of power. Some time before, the Comptroller, in one document, and the Supreme Court, in another, had already provided arguments on this issue against the government.

The Chilean reactionaries, like the United States when it seeks to camouflage its aggressions, no matter how transparent or barefaced these are, bestowed upon themselves legal pretexts.

Their words were *de jure*, their actions *de facto*.

September 11 was upon us.

NOTES

1

1. This is the national police force, virtually the fourth branch of Chile's armed forces.

2. *Foreign Relations of the United States, Diplomatic Papers, 1945: Vol. IX, The American Republics* (Department of State Publication 8452), pp. 733-755.

2

1. These statistics are taken from an Odeplan [the National Planning Organization] study. *Antecedents on the Development of Chile, 1960-1970* (Santiago, 1971).

2. Odeplan study, see note 1 above. It should be noted that, if the accumulated interest is added on, this debt was over $4 billion.

3

1. Roy Hansen, *Military Culture and Organizational Decline: A Study of the Chilean Army* (Ann Arbor, Michigan: University Microfilms, 1968).

2. This is an unofficial version; an official text does not exist, as far as I know.

3. Special Commission for Coordination in Latin America.

4. *Revista de derecho economico*, Universidad de Chile, last number 1970 and first number 1971.

5. *La Batalla del Cobre*, 1972.

6. Troncoso started the 1973 coup by rising in rebellion in Valparaiso, and then led the brutal repression in that port. Among his other functions, he is presently the junta's minister of housing.

4

1. The Inter-American Development Bank.

2. The Economic Commission for Latin America, and the Economic and Social Committee of the United Nations.

3. We should keep in mind that the term "CIA," instead of simply identifying the Central Intelligence Agency, has become synonymous with the entire U.S. apparatus for secret intelligence gathering, and now stands for a general policy of action. In spite of its important activities and its frequent acts of aggression abroad, the CIA is only one agency among all those that make up the U.S. espionage system. As far as Chile is concerned, the most important of these have been the Pentagon and its Defense Intelligence Agency (DIA).

4. From Edward Korry's testimony of March 27, 1973, to the Senate Special Subcommittee on Multinational Corporations of the Committee on Foreign Relations, chaired by Senator Frank Church: *Multinational Corporations and United States Foreign Policy: The*

International Telephone and Telegraph Company and Chile, 1970-71 (hereafter cited as *Multinational Corporations*), Part 1, pp. 277-318.

5. Memo from H. Hendrix and R. Berrellez to E. J. Gerrity, September 17, 1970. See *Multinational Corporations*, Part 2, Appendix II, pp. 608-615.

6. This article was accompanied by a reproduction of a visa request for nine officers, dated August 19, 1970.

5

1. See analysis by Anthony Sampson in his book, *The Sovereign State of ITT* (Greenwich, Connecticut: Fawcett Crest Book, 1974), pp. 270-271.

2. Cf. the following: E. J. Gerrity's cable to H. S. Geneen on September 29, 1970, *Multinational Corporations*, Part 2, Appendix II, pp. 626-628; the memo from Vice-President Gerrity to his colleague Merriam on September 30, *ibid.*, p. 636; Merriam's memos to Gerrity on October 7, *ibid.*, p. 643, and to McCone on October 9, *ibid.*, pp. 644-645; finally, McCone's declarations at the Senate hearings on March 21, 1973, *Multinational Corporations*, Part 1, pp. 93-125. (See also Sampson, *op. cit.*, pp. 272-275.)

3. Sampson, *op. cit.*, p. 268 (italics are Sampson's).

4. Memo from J. D. Neal to W. R. Merriam, September 21, 1970, *Multinational Corporations*, Part 2, Appendix II, p. 616.

5. Besides numerous direct Chilean sources, see memo from H. Hendrix and R. Berrellez to E. J. Gerrity, September 17, 1970, paragraph 8, *ibid.*, p. 610.

6. Once more, there are many statements on this. Among ITT memos that substantiate it are those by Hendrix and Berrellez to E. J. Gerrity on September 17, 1970, *ibid.*, pp. 608-615; by J. D. Neal to W. R. Merriam on September 21, *ibid.*, p. 616, and that of October 15, *ibid.*, pp. 656-658; and by Berrellez to Hendrix on November 13, 1970, *ibid.*, pp. 757-759.

7. *Ibid.*, Appendix I, p. 543.

8. During the week of September 16, I obtained a complete copy of the background briefing. It was given to the Chilean minister of foreign affairs, and is now in the hands of the junta. President Allende also obtained a copy for his personal archives, which, as far as I know, were destroyed when his office and home were pillaged. Though I am not able to quote Kissinger's words verbatim, many American and European journalists (among them Claude Julien, the Editor-in-Chief of *Le Monde Diplomatique*, and I. F. Stone) also had the opportunity to see the complete transcript, including the passage that referred to France and Italy.

9. One of the last commentaries, signed by Alberto Jacoviello, appeared in Rome's *L'Unita* in October 1973.

10. This "danger" was taken up by ITT on October 23, 1970, in W. R. Merriam's memo to Kissinger. See *Multinational Corporations*, Part 2, Appendix II, pp. 716-721.

11. On this, see ITT memos like the one sent on October 7 by Vice-President Merriam to fellow Vice-President Gerrity (*ibid.*, p. 643) and

which, according to a letter from Merriam to John McCone on the ninth (*ibid.*, pp. 644-648), contained a synopsis of a report Merriam had just received. In the memo of the seventh he says, "The lack of strong political activity on the part of Chile has hampered outsiders like the U.S. and Argentina in trying to help defeat Allende." [It's clear from the context that this refers to activities by the Chileans against Allende.] The synopsis enclosed with McCone's communication of October 9 literally says: "Another comment by State is that the failure of the Chileans, themselves, to react strongly against Allende is making it difficult for outsiders like the U.S. and Argentina to move in and try to stop Allende openly or covertly."

12. This plan was passed on to ITT Vice-President Gerrity by William Broe, head of the CIA's Latin American Division, on September 29, when the plan had already been under way for two weeks in Chile. (See September 29, 1970, cable from Gerrity to Geneen, *ibid.*, pp. 626-628.)

13. ITT memo for September 17 from Hendrix and Berrellez to E. J. Gerrity, previously cited (*ibid.*, pp. 608-615).

6

1. For instance, check the Hendrix and Berrellez memo of September 17, 1970, to E. J. Gerrity (*Multinational Corporations*, Part 2, Appendix II, pp. 611-613) for the conversations of the ITT agents on the thirteenth of that month with Arturo Matte, the top leader of the Right. Matte later admitted having participated, denying only (according to an AP dispatch from Santiago on March 23, 1973) that he had accepted any financial "contribution" offered by ITT. See also the ITT memo from J. D. Neal to W. R. Merriam, dated September 30, 1970 (*ibid.*, pp. 629-630), at the very moment the U.S. policy of subversion was being launched in Chile.

2. The Spanish word *aparecido*, which is used in the original, means "apparition" as well as "upstart."

7

1. Memo from Merriam to McCone, October 9, 1970, *Multinational Corporations*, Part 2, Appendix II, pp. 644-645.

2. Cf. Merriam's testimony before the Senate Subcommittee on March 20, 1973, *Multinational Corporations*, Part 1, pp. 4-52.

3. *Ibid.* See also, Anthony Sampson, *The Sovereign State of ITT* (Greenwich, Connecticut: Fawcett Crest Book, 1974) p. 277.

4. The reader should keep in mind that the following phrases are translated from the Spanish [Editor's note].

8

1. The Comptroller and the Supreme Court share the dubious privilege of being the only institutions of the whole public administration retained intact by the junta.

2. Agency for International Development

3. Overseas Private Investment Corporation

9

1. David Landau's book, *Kissinger: The Uses of Power*, cited in Chapter 7, is largely based on an analysis of these confidential statements of Kissinger.

2. Cf. the declaration of Chile's minister of economy to the Subcommittee of CIAP (Inter-American Committee of the Alliance for Progress) on Chile, April 1972.

3. The State Copper Corporation (Corporación del Cobre) and the State Development Corporation (Corporación de Fomento).

4. See Anthony Sampson, *The Sovereign State of ITT* (Greenwich, Connecticut: Fawcett Crest Book, 1974), p. 279.

5. A meeting of Chile with its creditors for the renegotiation of its foreign debt.

10

1. It should be noted that I was not present at these conversations, but was told of them by Deputy Maira and others who were.

2. The Dutch Communist who was blamed for the Reichstag fires.

3. General Carlos Prats was killed by a bomb blast as he was driving his car in Buenos Aires, Argentina, on September 30, 1974. He had been in Argentina since the coup [Editor's note].

4. The "Cordones Industriales" are formed by industrial workers from various "bands" of factories around Chile's larger cities; and the Communal Councils consist of many organizations, in addition to representatives from factories and farms who, among other things, pressure the government to distribute primary necessities in their areas.

INDEX

155